With Out Papers

Americanization of Italian Immigrants

my dear Cousin
Agnes
God Bless
Love Mary
Ann Tantalo

Anna Maria Tantalo

Anna Maria Tantalo

With Out Papers by Anna Maria Tantalo
Copyright © 2003

LCCN: 2004094528
ISBN: 0-9755779-0-5
1st Printing 2004

Printed in the United States of America
TriState Litho, Kingston, New York

Our Ancestors' Strength

At first reading this account may seem biographical
and it is to some extent. However, it is meant to be
an awakening of what has been lost by the Italian,
Polish, German, Irish and many other immigrants.
This is an effort to recapture the spirit and rekindle
the fire of our grandparents and parents.

European immigrants lived through religious
intolerance and scorn for the foreign born. Twentieth
century immigrants successfully mounted countless
hurdles. One of the most challenging was trying to
learn a foreign language while searching
employment during the depression.

ACKNOWLEDGEMENTS

I am grateful to my many relatives and friends that encouraged me to continue writing and travel despite my sudden loss of sight.

I want to express special gratitude to Sister Rosemary Howarth, Superior General of the School Sisters of Notre Dame. Unforgettable was the optimistic reception received from Sister Rosemary and all members of the motherhouse community in Rome. The motherhouse in Rome became my home base for research and gathering data from surrounding towns and villages.

Let me express some words of gratitude to Sister Stephen Marie Mahoney, SSND, for the painstaking proofreading of this work.

Sister Catherine O'Connell, former Provincial Leader, I am grateful for the time you spent reading the pre edited book.

Sister Joan Doyle, SSND, thanks for frequently enquiring on the progress of the writing.

Thank you Doctor Peter Liggett, retina specialist, for giving me the go ahead to write, travel, or whatever it took to complete my work.

I express my gratitude to Sister Bernadette Walsh, SSND for her readiness for granting my needed requests.

Jane Canestrini, thank you for making the workplace the perfect comfort spot.

Many thanks to Sister Joyce Wittman for taking on tasks needed to compile this work.

I appreciate the three high school students, Stephanie, Courtney, and Gina for reading assigned chapters so willingly and enthusiastically.

Thanks, Stella Calabrese, director of Casa Italiana at Nazareth College, Rochester, for providing signing sessions.

CONTENTS

1
Leaving the Old Country, Italy

Mary, a newly professed nun, of a semi-cloistered order, knelt next to her father near the mother's casket. It was her first visit to family since she had left her home four years previously. After a short prayer, they both rose and Lorenzo turned to his daughter and said, "Your mother is so young and was just a little sixteen year old girl when we married."

The daughter silently moved to sit with the group seated on rows of chairs provided for family members. Reminiscent of her childhood, her memory triggered a panoramic vision of home life. She recalled many scenes when she, along with her sisters, gathered around their mother, Josephine. The mother was a great storyteller and vividly retold over and over again her experiences both as a child and as a young bride.

Peppina, as Josephine was often called, was the second of five children. Frail but energetic, this child often followed her father, Dominic, on Sundays after Mass to stroll with him along the countryside. La Villa, a small Italian village, was nestled amid the high mountains bordering the National Park, east of Rome. These were beautiful times for the little girl. She loved to gaze at the high, high mountains and then stoop to pick up wild violets to present as a bouquet to her mother on the return home. Dominic, the tall red headed handsome man, would pick up the child as they approached their lovely newly built small home. Her father often coughed and on one particular Sunday, he seemed to cough almost constantly.

That was a vivid day for the five children. The parents were very somber. Dominic, with a loving look, spoke first,

"I am leaving for Rome tomorrow" he said softly, "but I will return soon. Remember to do your tasks, study and above all remember to pray."

Several days passed, and not soon enough, for Dominic's children and wife, Prudence. The news would not be good, his wife surmised, he looked much too pale and not at all his boisterous self. Dominic's wife immediately urged him to sit at the kitchen table and she would get some food ready. Prudence needed the time to calm herself before she could take bad news.

"Doctors in Rome said they don't have a cure for me but some medicine men in Rochester, New York, are doing fine work with people that have tuberculosis. They think I have TB as it is called in America. Patients are housed in buildings specifically for the disease. I'll get in touch with Francisco and get some advice from him."

Maria, the eldest of five children, left to summon Francisco, the village engineer, to come to their home. These were close neighbors. The engineer often called on Dominic to work with him as chief carpenter of projects he was engaged in. His wife, Filomena, was the head teacher of the village school, loved by the children and addressed "Signora", a title of distinction.

The children were often included in family conversations and Josephine sat quietly and motioned the others to do likewise. She did so want to know what was happening to her dear father. Village children were well trained to respect parents and elders, seldom questioning directives of parents. Shortly after, a meal was placed before Dominic and Prudence said,

"I would like you to be with us here but if there is the chance of a cure I am in favor of a trip to the Doctors in America. We can get along fine. The children are good and they will be busy with studies and helping with tasks at home. Time will go fast, we will miss you very much, but be joyful when you are free of that painful cough."

Francisco and his wife appeared at the door and were immediately ushered into the room. Because Dominic was finished with his meal he rose to meet his friends and glancing for approval from his wife, escorted Francisco to the parlor. I was not unusual for the two wives to spend time together chatting. The two young boys, Lazarus and John became restless and went outdoors to join friends. Since Prudence didn't ask the girls to leave, they remained waiting with expressions of anxiety not common on the faces of these happy girls.

"The news is not good, Filomena," said Prudence. "The doctors have no cure for Dominic in Rome. The doctors suggested he travel to America where some doctors are curing people with coughs as my husband's. It is not going to be easy for me to let him go away, but it is the only answer I can think of."

Filomena looked at her dear friend and said, "Let's wait to hear what the men have to say. Let us spend a little time at prayer." The women said a decade of the rosary and then resumed their conversation. Prudence was consoled at the words of her friend.

"You will not be alone in this. We are good friends and the neighbors hold this family in high esteem. What ever the men decide we will agree to." The women continued their conversation and the softness of their voices made the girls realize it was time for them to leave.

As the young are accustomed to do, they kept speculating on what would happen to them. It was Maria's chance to tell her sisters what she had been considering for a while. Recalling the incident of her fall from a horse which resulted in a limp, she told her sisters how much she minded being crippled, therefore, did not want to continue school after completing studies at la Signora's school.

"I will not go away to school and let strange girls shun me. I feel safe with the village girls. They knew me when I, too, could walk nice and even dance." Maria stubbornly stated.

"Papa will never let you do that," said Antonia, youngest of the three girls. Tonia, as she was often called, was the sensitive one, always ready to sympathize and help. It was apparent this child was frightened and feared the future.

"America is a nice country and I think papa should go there for a cure and we could all go, too. Mama's brother, John Baptist, went to America a few years ago. Our cousin Sophia likes living in the United States. In her last letter, she mentioned going to school in Rochester and boys and girls go to the same school. I'm sure I will like America." Suddenly, the girls could hear movement of chairs in the parlor and went to join their mother. They were allowed to remain, sat down while the men folks settled down and Maria went into the side room returning with a pitcher of wine. The other two followed her example and went for glasses and cookies.

The discussion that followed was serious. Dominic told his wife that Francisco was urging him to go to the Rochester sanitarium and try for the cure. Francisco in turn, assured Prudence that he had heard of the work the doctors were doing there. A friend's relative was cured after a two-year treatment. He would have a difficult time replacing Dominic but was willing to wait for his return. Francisco said that he would like to spend some time in the village. So much of his work took him and fellow villagers away from family.

"I am sure there are many projects right here in La Villa that need tending to," said Francisco. A joyful expression shone on Filomena's face. Many of the engineer's projects took him to far away places. Many were the long nights and lonely days that filled Filomina's life. Her children were away at schools, and although they came home often, her times alone were many.

After the departure of their two friends, Dominic turned to his wife and said, "We are fortunate to have such good and loyal friends. What do you think Prudence?"

There would be no doubt as to the answer. "Francisco is right. You need to at least investigate the cure they offer in Rochester, New York. I'll write John Baptist and ask for housing for you. He, too, will prove to be a good friend."

Several days of discussions and planning followed. Often the dialogue included just the two parents and after a major specific decision had been made all the children were included in the final arrangements. It was an exciting and special time for the family and the reality of separation didn't occur until the final day of departure approached.

Villagers, hearing of the departure of Dominic, gathered at the home with wishes for a safe trip and promised to pray for him. He was driven away in a horse drawn carriage accompanied by his dear friend, Francisco. It was decided Filomana would remain with Prudence and her children until the return of Francisco. The departure would be from Rome and both men knew the city well, but it was Filomana who suggested her husband go with his friend and remain with Dominic until he boarded the boat.

Family life took on the usual routine with the expected gaps of times when the father was missed. Sundays and evenings were the times the children and wife felt the absence most. Often though, Prudence would read a letter she had received from her husband. At first most of the news centered around Dominic's getting settled as a boarder at the home of John Baptist's friend. There were also letters detailing his visits to the doctors and waiting for prognosis on his disease and what the future might hold. There seemed to be some uncertainty about his illness.

Finally a letter came that seemed to sadden the mother of these five children. They, too, seemed less boisterous and noisy. Dominic had a doctor that he trusted and was willing to follow his advice. The news was the father was not eligible for the Iola Sanitarium. His disease was truly a lung disease but not contagious and not TB. The doctor said he would be willing to continue to treat him if he remained in Rochester. The prognosis was that it was a terminal illness and with an unpredictable number of years he would be able to continue working.

Since Dominic had acquired a good inside job, it would be better for him to remain where he was. The engineering jobs in Italy required travel, long working days and many times their father worked outdoors during inclement weather. Dominic cautioned Prudence a quick decision would be foolish.

"Let's wait at least six months," suggested Dominic. "We will wait for termination of treatments as well as test checks, evaluate what they reveal and then make decisions. Let us ask Francisco for his opinion and consult with doctors in Rome. Francisco will get in touch with the doctors. I have already written him. In the mean time we will pray that God's will be done. We need to think of the children and what is not burdensome for you, my dear."

Josephine and Maria were especially concerned about their mother. They could perceive worry lines on her usually serene and happy countenance. Maria and Josephine spent time discussing the situation and finally one day Maria spoke confidentially and softly to Josephine.

"Peppina, I know that you may not agree with me but mama is worrying about finances. She was looking at the account book last evening and that worried expression came over her face. Several times I mentioned that I would not continue my education after completing La Signora's school.

If I remain at home and do sewing I can bring in some money and it will help."

Josephine hugged her sister and replied,

"Maria, I know what you mean and I have thought of the same thing. Tonia should continue even after she completes her present phase of education but I agree that it would be a good thing to help with finances."

Maria took up her domineering stance.

"We will wait until this evening after the others have gone to bed. I'll bring up the subject of education and give my reason. I'll tell mama that it will be embarrassing for me to go to a new school limping along and accepting the taunts from other strange girls. Our mother will understand how I feel and I'll not mention finances. Don't say anything about your schooling just yet. You still have some time before you complete your studies at the village school."

Dominic's letters from America came regularly once a week. It seems that much of his Sundays were spent writing family. The letters fascinated the children. After she read the letter herself several times, Prudence would gather the children in the parlor and read the glowing accounts of life in America. The letters seemed cheerful and hopeful.

John Baptist invited his brother in law to spend time with family. John had been in America several years, knew the language and had a fine job. His three daughters and son hungered for news of the little village in Italy where they were born and had spent happy childhood days. Dominic and John talked often of the possibility of Dominic remaining in the

United States. Finally, the day came when the father and husband wrote that he had acquired a fine job with the blessings of his doctor. It was an inside job in a nice newly built furniture factory. He was hired as a cabinetmaker.

Soon letters included a check with instructions to Prudence that it be used for expenses and education of the children. The family fell into a comfortable routine and the day arrived for the end of the school year. It was then that Maria told her mother she would not continue her education. Prudence was quickly persuaded. She was a compassionate lady and so concerned about her eldest daughter. There was little tolerance at that time for women that were unmarried. Little was offered in the workplace. Most young women looked forward to finding a suitable partner and raising a family. Would Maria be able to attract a partner with her disability? Most men wanted a healthy wife that would be a worthy and able mother to children.

Summer time went by quickly and the children were getting ready for the start of school. A number of villagers received the news that Old Rose was teaching Maria to be a dressmaker. This young girl was not only a good seamstress but also knew how to sew a fashionable garment for the young women. There was no let up on orders. Josephine expressed her desire to learn dressmaking, too. Prudence reminded her daughter that Dominic wanted the girls to be educated. The following year Josephine decided that she, too, would not go away to school. The money could be saved for future needs of the family.

A strange happening alarmed Prudence. Letters stopped arriving. Old letters were reread many times but still no new letters came. During one of the many visits to her friend's home, Filomena was told of the strange stoppage of mail. Filomena assured Prudence and told her that she would consult her husband. After a few weeks, a letter finally arrived.

Dominic wrote that he had decided after praying, consulting his friends, Francisco and John Baptist, he would be making his home in America. He needed his family with him and told his wife it would be good if she planned to board a boat early summer. John Baptist seemed to know about traveling. It was John that suggested early summer for the trip. No reason was given why Dominic stopped writing his weekly letters to wife and family. It was Filomena that one day told Prudence that Francisco questioned Dominic. The answer given was,

"I sent money home to use for their needs and for the education of the girls. Prudence knows how I value education. We talked about that often and agreed the girls needed to be educated, too."

"Francisco explained to your husband that it was only out of concern for him and it is good for family members to make sacrifices for ill or needy members. After all, he told Dominic, children should learn at an early age that when one family member is needy all must come to the rescue."

In telling of the event to her daughters she said that the subject never came up again.

The months and days that followed were hectic, busy, and filled with changing emotions. Maria did not want to go and dreaded the thought of leaving their beautiful home and lovely town. The boys were delighted and excited.

Tonia couldn't make up her mind but Josephine was definitely overjoyed. She was anxious to meet her cousins. Josephine and her cousin Sophia were now exchanging letters often. Prudence was silent and preoccupied. However, as the time approached for leaving the town, Dominic's family talked almost constantly of the joy that would be theirs when they were united with their father again.

Boat travel was the only mode of travel across waters. Decisions had to be made as to what should be taken with them to the new country. Villagers were all anxious to advise them. Many suggested linens would not be needed. Others suggested jewelry would not be fashionable in America. Many knew little of American customs and imagined all sorts of strange behavior that their friends would encounter. As was her custom, Prudence sought advice from her friend, Filomena.

Francisco accompanied Filomena on one of the visits and gave some specific instructions on travel. He and his wife would travel with them to Rome and make sure that all would go well for the long oversea trip. They would be going by steamboat and Francisco told Prudence he would send over two steamer trunks for them. He had used them long ago and had no need of them. The day of travel finally arrived. The children and Prudence dressed in what Filomena suggested. The day of departure was a beautiful spring day and the trip to Rome was in a horse drawn carriage. Their baggage followed in a wagon driven by two family friends.

They waited in line to board the ship. People boarding all seemed to speak different languages and seemed so foreign to the children. As the line shortened they waved goodbye to their friends and immediately Prudence walked tall. She suddenly had that take-charge expression. The two older girls reached for the hands of the younger boys, and then followed their mother and Tonia closely.

It was late afternoon and they were ushered to their room with several bunk beds. The surroundings seemed so strange and all were a little frightened. The basket of food that they had taken with them was a welcome sight. After a hearty meal sleep overtook them. The serenity of that first night did not occur again until they finally arrived in New York City.

It was a difficult trip. All got seasick with the exception of Lazarus and Tonia. Josephine remembered it as such an endless and painful trip. Lazarus had fun with some of the sailors but Tonia was constantly caring for the other members of the family that were so ill. Lazarus, Tonia assured her mother, was helping with the clean ups and was very obedient and listened carefully to instructions.

A young woman noticed the young Italian girl and offered to help her. She, too, was traveling with her family but had made the trip before. Jenny and her mother were returning from a visit to her grandmother who lived near Naples. Her new friend was not only helpful but kept Tonia from worrying. She assured Tonia that many people became sick on sea trips.

"Of course, blondes do not have the same trouble as dark haired people do. Notice, Tonia, I am light haired and so are you and Lazarus. All other members of your family are dark haired and therefore will get sick."

That was such a comfort to Tonia and she no longer feared that the sick members of the family would die. Her smile returned and she lovingly administered to the members of her family cheerfully. Prudence smiled when her dear little girl gave the reason for her sickness. She was dark haired the daughter explained, and would be fine once they completed the ocean trip. "I'll go along with her thinking," thought Prudence. "The poor child needs something to keep up her courage." She cautioned the older girls not to contradict the child but just humor her along.

Jenny's mother, Angelina, visited and helped the young girl with the care of her daughter's new friends. She proved to be a great help to Prudence. They became friends immediately. It was Angelina that helped the family go through customs and her knowledge of English made not only getting through customs comfortable but she also stayed with her new friends until Dominic, John Baptist and John's wife Anna finally met them.

2
Becoming Americanized

Abandoning all reserve, Prudence tearfully and happily hugged her husband, brother and sister in law. The children's joy was uncontrollable. Their shouts, laughter and great show of emotions attracted the looks of other new arrivals and they smilingly tolerated the blocking of walks.

John Baptist lost no time in showing his sister and brother in law that he was familiar with New York. He led them all into one of the fine restaurants insisting they needed to sit for a good meal before continuing their train journey to Rochester. It was a welcome respite. It was their first exposure to American food. Josephine often spoke of her first introduction to the taste of pie.

"At the end of the meal we were served apple pie. I had never seen the likes of it. My first thought was that it would be pasta like concoction. What a surprise when it had a sweet taste."

It was a long train trip to their new home and the quiet drone of muffled voices of the adults made the children sleepy. Even Maria and Josephine lost interest when the conversation turned to mundane things such as house rental, talk of factory jobs and other unfamiliar stuff.

The train stopped at a noisy station with all kinds of people rushing around and talking loudly in strange languages. They entered a large building with elegant marble pillars and terrazzo floors. It was all so strange and a little like their first glance of Rome.

"This is Rochester," said John as he too quickened his steps and all were silently following their new uncle. "He must know everything," whispered Josephine to Tonia. The smiling face of Josephine brought relief to the little girl and she quickly reached up to grasp her sister's hand. The warmth of the hand brought great comfort to the child. With swinging arms the two walked along with the grown ups. With the passing of time, they began to look around to assess this new place that was to be their home forever.

The group of new immigrants arrived at a huge open area with cobble stone paths and many horse drawn wagons. Carriages were moving along the street. There seemed to be confusion as strange speaking people, mostly men, loudly shouted names of people they were searching for. Suddenly John Baptist, too, shouted, "Here we are."

Immediately, a large wagon appeared with two children and an adult.

Without even greeting the new comers, the man and children smiled and quickly picked up the luggage, they made their way to the wagon and deposited all the new comers' belongings. Uncle John as well as Aunt Anna joined them in loading the vehicle. As Dominic and Prudence reached to join them in loading, John placed a gentle hand on his brother in law's shoulder and assured him that the children and neighbor wanted to be helpful.

It was a strange looking wagon. Two benches ran across the front of the vehicle and the back had pillows tossed along the sides of the wagon. All the children sat on pillows but the grown ups sat in the front with the men leading the two strong horses. As Uncle John helped the children climb into the wagon he introduced the cousins. Their cousins, Sophia and young John spoke Italian and what a joy to the immigrant children that they could finally understand what some Americans were saying.

Young John and the two boys immediately moved to the back of the wagon, John explaining and acting the sightseeing guide. A few years older than the newcomers, he slowly explained the different types of vehicles that were being used in Rochester. He fascinated the youngsters and kept them interested during the whole trip to their new lodging.

Sophia, closer to Josephine's age and recalling the contents of their letters, she continued in a confidential manner. They would like their new neighborhood the cousin assured them. She knew some friends that lived in the house next door to where they were going to live.

"You will not always understand what your neighbors are saying but you will learn English quickly and will be able to speak to anyone that lives in America. "I know some English words," added Josephine.

"You never learned English at La Signora's school," retorted Maria.

"Well, you would not go to afternoon classes at La Signora's. Remember when I wasn't going to continue my education, Filomena invited us both to attend the afternoon and evening classes for the village girls that were not going away to school. You weren't interested and said that it was a waste of time." The conversation among the girls continued with news of the "old country" as Sophia kept using the term for their lovely village, La Villa.

"Where will we be living?" asked the practical Maria.

"Oh, you will be living in a rented house. That is where we lived before my father purchased a house on the next street. I'll be living very close to you and we can be together much of the time and I'll show you how the Americans live.

"What do you mean how the Americans live. Don't they live like we do?" interjected Maria.

"Well, you will become Americanized. You will be eating differently and going to schools that have boys and girls in the same class. Some times we even have men teachers."

"I'm not interested in school. I am a trained seamstress and have my very own sewing machine," said Maria.

"Oh, yes, continued Tonia, and she make such beautiful dresses. She even made a wedding gown."

It was evident that Sophia was impressed and was determined that she would be one of Maria's first customers.

"You will be making dresses for me then, too, won't you? I like the suit you are wearing. Did you make it?"

"Oh, yes" answered Maria kindly. "If your mother will supply the material and you know I do get paid. I am now old enough to help family and besides, I am going to start saving items for when I get married."

The younger girls exchanged looks and Josephine shrugged her shoulders.

"Do you have a man waiting for you to come back to Italy?" questioned Sophia.

"Not yet but some day I will. It is not too early to begin getting things put away."

"They call it a Hope Chest," informed the young cousin.

"I haven't started to save but my mother said that when I am fifteen years old she will buy me a beautiful trunk. My friend, Gemma, has already started hers but she is using an old box. I'll wait until my mother gives me a nice container."

Most of the remainder of the trip was spent discussing future possibilities.

Suddenly the wagon came to a halt and the children's conversations stopped. John and Sophia quickly rose and smiled at their cousins. The two jumped nimbly off the wagon and the young newcomers gazed around them. Uncle John immediately stood in front of a small cottage and motioned with his hand. This was their new dwelling they all realized. All silently scrutinized the house and small fenced yard.

"Why is there a fence in front of the house?" inquired Maria.

Uncle John again took complete control. Angelina watched the face of her sister in law, waiting for approval.

Prudence smiled and the children followed her example.

As they approached the front entrance several women were waiting and with outstretched arms, greeted Prudence, their long ago friend from the Old Country. All the men folks as well as the two young boys immediately picked the luggage and carried the bags to one of the rooms. Aunt Ann took Prudence by the hand and led the mother and daughters on a tour of their new house. The place they were led to was a small room with a bathtub, sink, toilet and small stand holding a large number of towels. It was bright with sun streaming through a skylight.

Prudence's sister in law softly whispered to the relatives, "This is a treasure. Many of the homes here in America do not have a sala de bain. They have a shed outdoors and call it a backhouse." The tour continued until they arrived into the kitchen. Places were set and the smell of food predominated. John was to remain with his sister's family and after the neighbors showed Prudence where the food was, they all departed. Anna assured Prudence she would return in a short time and continue to answer questions that they might have.

Prudence immediately became the lady of the house, calling on Maria to help her serve and instructed the others to be seated so that they could eat and then get ready for evening company. They all needed to change their clothing, unpack the suitcases and trunks. It was assuring to young Tonia. She was still bewildered at the entire goings on. The child liked the tone her mother was using, it sounded so much like it did when they were home in LaVilla.

Anna arrived with Sophia but young John was left home. "The two young boys must be tired and should be put to bed," suggested Anna. Prudence agreed and Dominic let the two boys to their bedrooms. They were tired and needed little persuasion. Maria led the girls to investigate the bedrooms. Company did not linger long. This newly united family finally had a long and restful sleep.

3
Educating Immigrants

Life for this new Italian family in Rochester began to take some semblance of normalcy. However, many changes were constantly taking place in the lives of the children. Josephine could hear her parents softly discussing the schools they should be attending in the fall.

Happiness did prevail among the members of Dominic's family. To see the father and husband daily gave this family great joy. Her sister in law introduced Prudence to a lunch pail. "Here in America workers take a lunch with them. Best to prepare lunch in the evening as men leave the house very early. Workers leave their homes as soon as they hear the factory whistles blow at 6 A.M. Give your man a good breakfast, too," advised Anna. Happy shouts of children and a smiling wife met Dominic on his return home evenings.

With help of other Italians in the neighborhood, Prudence was introduced to the near by grocery store and meat market. Food didn't change as much as Sophia had warned. There were several disputes over the purchase of meat and other luxury items such as fresh fruit.

"My health seems to be improving and I am able to work," Dominic assured his wife. "We all need good food to keep us healthy. If you recall, I did tell you that some of my wages are placed in a bank. The money earns interest and can be withdrawn when the need arises. Money that is given to you on pay day is to be used for food and clothing."

Prudence reminded herself that this was a proud man and realized money distribution was his domain. True, her husband seemed to be in better health. He no longer had the pallor and the cough had subsided. This wife was a thrifty woman, she spent wisely and made sure there was no waste in the home. Even the crumbs from the table were given to the birds. Washing and drying dishes were tasks for the older girls but Tonia swept the floor and shook the tablecloth out in the backfield. Tonia often lingered to watch flocks of birds feast on crumbs and bits of bread. Mrs.

Miller, a neighbor and bird lover, taught the child names of birds. Most of them were tiny sparrows and robins.

As the summer sped quickly by, Prudence and her husband began discussing school possibilities for the children. Strong debates on the education of Josephine began. Josephine pleaded with her father to wait until she knew the English language better. Dominic, after reflecting on his own problem with the language, told his daughter to stay at home, study and help Prudence with household chores.

Dominic and Prudence called on the pastor of St. Patrick's Church. The priest, Father O'Hern, was acquainted with Dominic and had often stopped to enquire about his health when this young Italian man first came to Rochester. Father O'Hern had studied in Rome, therefore, knew the Italian language well. This was their parish and they attended Mass at the beautiful cathedral. Shortly after their arrival, Prudence and the children began attending daily mass. On one of the mornings when Father O'Hern was outside the rectory, the group of Italian immigrants started a conversation with the priest. He urged the Mother to register the children for school. He walked them to the school where registration was taking place. Tonia, Lazarus and John became students of St. Patrick's school.

Young John, their cousin, was busy with high school studies and didn't visit his cousins often but Sophia and the two older sisters, Armina and Grace, visited them often. Uncle John's daughters found work at Fashion Park, a clothing factory. They entertained the Cocuzzi girls with their stories of events at the factory.

"Pepina, you must come and work with us. You will like it and make money," invited Sophia.

"I can't speak English and wouldn't know what to do," answered Josephine.

"Many of the bosses are either Italian or other nationalities. They know what problems newcomers have and they are always willing to get one of the girls that speaks the same language to instruct a new worker. One of us could be assigned to work with you. Of course, if we work together, we may not waste time but keep on working. We do piece work, get paid only for the work we do and what passes inspection," added her cousin.

Continued accounts of her cousin's workplace encouraged Josephine to apply for a job at the factory. Prudence listened to Maria and Josephine discussing factory work and she instantly became concerned. Their mother realized how difficult it would be to persuade Dominic. He was determined his girls should be educated. On quiet evenings, Prudence and her husband talked of the children's future. Her husband often discussed factory work including women working there. It was not a good picture he painted.

"Men do not respect female worker and frequently use unsavory language in their presence. Our girls will never work in factories," determined Dominic.

One Sunday afternoon, while John Baptist's family was visiting the Cocuzzi family, Sophia spoke up and said for all to hear, "Pipina, the forelady said for you to come to Fashion

Park one day this week. You will apply for a job and Gemma said that you can start work immediately."

A brief period of silence followed but the children were not aware that something was amiss. Several times, when the adults visited, Dominic always dismissed the suggestion from Anna that the girls could go to work in the factory where her daughters were employed. Factory work for the girls ceased to be mentioned after some strong rejecting statements from Prudence's husband.

Soon after their cousins' family left, Josephine spoke up determinedly, "What shall I wear when I go to Fashion Park tomorrow?"

With a soft but very firm intonation, Dominic replied, "No daughter of mine will work in a factory and be subjected to the taunts and obscenities of uncouth men."

Josephine froze and realized this definitely was no time to plead with her father. Leaving the presence of the silent members of the family, the young girl tearfully left the room and slammed the door as she entered her bedroom. Sobs could be heard as the boys left for outdoor play while Maria, Tonia and Prudence began clearing the table, quietly completing tasks around the kitchen and dining room. Dominic picked up the newspaper and silently read the news. It was a sobering time for Dominic and Prudence. "These American children are going to choose their own paths on their journey to adulthood," reflected Prudence.

It was the boys' boisterous entrance into the kitchen that helped dispel the tension of the dramatic clash of opinions between a father's protective concern and the demands of a lively growing girl.

"The ice cream cart is passing by. May we have money for ice cream cones?" shouted the two boys in unison.

Dominic reached into his pocket and instructed the boys to buy cones of ice cream for them all. When John and Lazarus returned with the treat they distributed the cones. It was Lazarus who gently knocked on the closed door of Josephine's room. He opened the door and whispered, "Don't be upset, dada worries about us all the time and he is not as strong as he pretends." Maria followed and took the cone from her brother, thanked him for getting them the treat and shut the door after him.

"Don't cry, Josephine, Maria said. "Papa will change his mind after a while. He always gives in to you in the end. You know how to persuade him."

"Why do I always have to work so hard to persuade dada to my way of thinking. He treats me like a child. You can work, have your own sewing machine and even go visiting alone. Every time I leave the house, dada asks you to go along. Doesn't he trust me?"

"No, that is not it at all. You are very pretty and fathers worry about their daughters." With that, Maria said gently, "I have a surprise for you. I'll be back with it right away." With the quick exit and just as speedy return, Maria walked into the room with Prudence and Tonia, then presented Pepina with a lovely light blue velvet dress. "This is a surprise for you from mama. She wanted you to have a new dress for Sundays. Do you like it?" Hugs and laughter followed. Prudence uttered a silent prayer of thanksgiving. She knew the clash would come and was truly fearful.

Prudence returned to the parlor, picked up her prayer book to silently sit next to her husband. Dominic smiled gently at his wife and he, too, thanked God for this wife who was truly a very good wife and mother.

Mornings, after the children left for school, Maria and Josephine accompanied their mother to St. Patrick's Church for daily morning Mass. The girls always looked forward to days when Father O'Hern would be watering flowers in the rectory front yard. The girls would call out in English "Good morning Father." The priest would cheer and laugh and always gave them a new English phrase to learn. Josephine of course, confided to father on one of the mornings, that her father thought girls who worked in factories were bad.

The priest gave one of his boisterous laughs and replied. "You are very fortunate girls to have a father that is not going to have you work for long hours for so little pay. Maria is earning enough money for three by just using God's gifts. Fathers are proud and they do not want women to be burdened with earning money. They want to be the family providers. There are many womanly tasks that can be learned at your mother's side. Needle work, cooking, cleaning is always best learned at home."

"He is such a fine priest isn't he mama?" added Maria as they continued on their way home.

"Priests are a great blessing. They teach us about God and how to live a life that will bring us not only great blessings in this life but prepare us to meet our Maker. We have received many blessings and graces as family and I pray daily that one of the boys will enter the seminary."

"Mama, Lazarus is very handsome, is a good student and will one day have a fine job. My friends really like him and he will surely marry one day. John likes a good time and often talks of being a sales man," responded Maria.

"Well, God's will be done," Prudence, replied.

"How fast these children are growing with Lazarus now as tall and handsome as his father. John worries me, Dominic does not seem to correct him as much as he did Lazarus. He must be too tired and weary at the end of the day. He didn't say much when I told him that his youngest son often arrives late for school. Although he leaves early enough, he stops and visits shops on the way to school. John likes to chat with storekeepers and shows more interest in job possibilities rather than studies," reflected Prudence.

"We no longer have children, Prudence," commented Dominic one Sunday afternoon. It had become routine for the Cocuzzi children to join friends. Lazarus and John either were playing baseball with their teams or watching games at the near by Brown's Square Park. Maria and Josephine joined their cousins and spent Sundays strolling along Main and State Streets. Many of Maria's dress pattern ideas were gleaned from looking at the dress displays in the store windows.

"Something has been taking up much of my thoughts lately," confided Dominic. "This house has served us well but it is much too small. One of my fellow workers, a German friend at work, is leaving America. His ailing parents need him at home. He has a large house on one of the side streets. We can afford to buy it and you would like it Prudence. I saw it yesterday on the way home from work. It has a large porch, plenty of room and a large back yard. Nice place for planting tomatoes and lettuce. Best of all, it has a separate section upstairs. It's a beautiful afternoon, the house is close by and we could walk by it. When you see it, you can judge if you would like to live there."

"This is an amazing man, I married," thought Prudence. "He is always confronting me with surprises."

It was a stroll that the mother remembered for a long time and would frequently like to recount it to her girls. Her daughters were very American and romantic. When she told of the incident, Tonia always remarked, "DaDa loved you very much mama." This house on a tree-lined street became the home of this happy family. The separate section with an outdoor stair entrance puzzled Prudence.

"That is an ideal part of the house Maria can use. It has an entrance for her clients and a nice sewing room could be made of the adjoining space. We could keep the house on Broad Street for John and this house would belong to Lazarus. Maria's quarters could be converted into your own separate apartment after I am gone. You would be close to Lazarus and John but yet have your own little place," confided Dominic.

These new young adults loved their new Romayne Street home where they spent happy days learning the American way.

4
Unionizing Industries

Rochester, New York was fast growing into a city with constantly changing face. It was now being called the Flour City as well as the flower City. New factories were beginning to spring up and recently another like industry, the DAISY FLOUR MILL, joined THE BIG B FlOUR. Flower gardens still abounded but streets were busy with many horse drawn commercial wagons.

Romeyn Street was away from their Broad Street home and therefore was a quiet tree lined street with small front yards that often included flowerbeds. Italians treasured this rich soil, therefore, their backyards became large vegetable gardens where they planted tomatoes, lettuce, peppers and like vegetables, using most of the space for favorite food plants and herbs.

Prudence loved her new home and she liked to play hostess to newcomers in the neighborhood. Many Italians from her home village were coming to Rochester. These new immigrants immediately sought out their old friends and were grateful for the help, advice and friendship. This was a family that had settled and was comfortable in this foreign land.

Young people gathered at the Cocuzzi home. Included in the group were friends of Tonia, John and Lazarus. These younger members of the family began inviting school friends and English began to dominate much of the conversation. Maria and Josephine, however, were not as ready to switch to the new language but continued to speak Italian, which made Prudence feel comfortable with the young.

Among the visitors to the house on Romeyn Street were young men from the old country, seeking advice about lodging, work and other information pertinent to the immigrants, seeking a place in this new vast country with fertile land. Many of them searched for friends that wrote glowing accounts of their newly adopted homeland. A few came just for curiosity. Others were serious about making America their permanent home.

Included in this group of newly arrived countrymen, was Lorenzo Tantalo, son of Filomena and Francisco, old time friends of Dominic and Prudence. At his first visit, Lorenzo told Dominic that he had completed his basic education, completed his military time, and wanted to visit America before he returned to Italy. He explained that he was interested in industry and curious about the attraction it held for so many of his friends. Most of his conversations initially centered around his returning to Rome for studies.

After a few months stay, Lorenzo found employment at one of the factories. At first he was curious and wanted to know how business operated. An industrialist, young George Kondolf, urged Lorenzo to start up a bank exchange for the Italian immigrants. Mr. Kondolf suggested that it would be a great service to his countrymen. Lorenzo began studying English and started a small bank exchange at one of the spaces on the first floor of the hotel on the corner of Oak and Smith Street. This city where the young Italian found many fascinating choices soon became the place that Lorenzo finally selected as his permanent home. It dimmed his desire to continue studies. However, this young man did miss his family and homeland, consequently, he habitually filled the void by spending time at the Cocuzzi home.

It was on one sunny warm Sunday afternoon that Lorenzo found Prudence and Dominic sitting alone in the living room. He immediately confided that America would become his home and he was interested in courting Josephine.

"You are a fine young man, Lorenzo, come from a good family and I am sure you have a brilliant future to look forward to. We are honored that you are interested in one of our daughters. Josephine, however, is much too young, only fifteen years old but Maria is eighteen and would also make a good wife. Maria needs to be the first to marry. Consider Maria as a possible fiancée."

The man was surprised at the request but remained silent and went on to discuss news of home and other matters. Visits to the Cocuzzi family continued as usual for several weeks. In the mean time the young Italian was determined to hope that Josephine would be his wife. He finally planned to get a suitor for Maria, thinking that it would solve the problem of having Maria marry first.

Several young immigrants were also living at the same boarding house where Lorenzo resided. He decided that he needed to approach one of his own countrymen. Frank Serafine, also an Italian, came from the same village and was a hard working, stable young fellow. Lorenzo approached Frank one evening, after his friend was complaining about the food at the boarding house and said he was thinking of moving.

"You need a good wife, Frank, confided Lorenzo. "I'm thinking of getting married and have my own home soon. Why don't you come with me to visit the Cocuzzi family? There are three lovely girls in the family and I'm sure that Dominic would be happy to have you court Maria. She is not promised to anyone yet. I plan to marry Josephine and I think Tonia is much too young. Maria is a good woman, a seamstress and I'm sure would make a fine wife."

"I don't make enough money to marry and besides I don't want any responsibility just yet," answered Frank.

Lorenzo finally persuaded Frank to accompany him. He made sure that they would arrive at a time when they would be invited to Sunday dinner. These two young men appeared early one Sunday morning. Lorenzo commented as he was ushered into the home,

"We attended the early Mass this morning and thought we could stop for a short visit before going home."

"Do stay for dinner", pleaded Prudence as the young men walked into the living room.

Dominic, as was his custom, greeted the men, encouraged them to have a glass of wine and asked for news of the old country. As the men chatted and waited for dinner, Dominic engaged them in conversations that included some personal questions directed to Frank. The Serafine family was a well known respected family of LaVilla. It was Maria who came in to ask if the men wanted additional wine. Both men smiled but declined the offer. Soon both men were led into the dining room where a delicious Italian dinner was served. Frank was beaming with contentment as he enjoyed food that he had been longing for. This started a new trend that included the two young men visiting the Cocuzzi home often.

One evening, both Lorenzo and Frank appeared at the home of Dominic and Prudence. Lorenzo, ever the spokesman, asked if he could see Dominic privately. Dominic led them into the parlor and after Prudence brought in a pitcher of wine and glasses, Lorenzo made a request,

"We are asking for a special honor, Dominic," said Lorenzo. "I am sure that you must know that we are both good providers, religious men and want to court your daughters Josephine and Maria. Frank would make a good husband for Maria and I will try to be worthy of Josephine."

Dominic was not surprised as he and his wife often discussed the sudden appearance of Frank Serafine. Both agreed that these were good men and as Prudence's husband explained, "I will feel more at ease if our daughters are married before I become seriously ill." The girls' father answered, "Yes, you are fine young men and I'm sure you will make every effort to be good husbands. There is one request I need to make before I agree. Josephine is too young now; she can be courted but must wait until she is sixteen to marry. When you discuss plans, the wedding date must be put off until after Josephine is of age." The men both quickly acknowledged that it was a reasonable request. After the blessing of the father, they quietly sipped their glasses of wine.

These men told Dominic they had planned to arrive at the home with horse and carriage the next Sunday. They would make their intentions known to the girls while visiting the nearby Highland Park. With that, the men departed, leaving Dominic and Prudence the task of relaying the news to their daughters. Maria, was overjoyed. However, Josephine was not only surprised but also immediately objected. She felt that she needed time to work before she thought of marriage.

Dominic, of course, instantly assured her that work was not an acceptable future, even if it was part time. With that he dismissed the discussion and left Prudence with the girls. Maria and Prudence pleaded with Josephine but the young girl continued to withhold her agreement. For several days, Maria pleaded with tears, "I have been dreaming that some day I would marry. Here is a chance that at last I could have a normal life like other women but you just will not accept any reasonable request." The tears moved Josephine and finally agreed to go along for the ride but assured Maria that she had doubts about the arrangement.

During their rides, Lorenzo always took along letters he had received from his family. After taking the reins, before leading the horses along the park paths, Lorenzo handed Josephine the letters. He encouraged Josephine to read them aloud so that they could hear news of the old country.

Josephine was especially interested, fascinated and began looking forward to these Sunday rides. The times spent together with her sister encouraged Maria and she capitalized on these accounts assuring Josephine that she was fortunate to be part of such a fine family. Letters contained accounts of Filomena's work with Dr. Maria Montessori, the brain surgeon. The doctor was working with educators to devise methods that would stimulate brain damaged children. These new teaching methods brought the world of learning to these unfortunate students that were neglected and grew up to be academically stunted because of untapped resources.

When the Cocuzzi girls met with their cousins or friends, Maria gave glowing accounts of the contents of the letters that were read during their Sunday afternoons. Sophia, Josephine's closest friend and cousin, would often ask Josephine to recount the contents of the letters and news of the old country. Slowly, Josephine began to enjoy the conversations, letters and company of her partner.

Maria was quick to seize the opportunity and began gathering materials for hope chests for both herself and her sister. Time passed quickly and on a bright fall day, Aunt Anna arrived at the Cocuzzi home, announcing to Prudence and the girls,

"I will be going to a nearby furniture store and will be purchasing cedar chests for my girls. Prudence, why don't you and the girls come along? Maria and Josephine should purchase now, too, as they are having a sale at the H.B. Graves furniture store. Beautiful chests were displayed and we saw them as we went window shopping last Sunday."

Prudence quickly went for her shawl and commanded the girls to do likewise, then without reflection or comments, Josephine and Maria followed their Aunt and mother. When they arrived at the store, an Italian sales woman stepped forward and was an expert at selling these items to future brides.

A large stack of chests was a few feet away and Maria hastened in the direction, holding Josephine's hand. She exclaimed gleefully,

"Mama, look at these beautiful wooden chests."

Always alert for a buyer, the sales lady came forward and informed the women,

"These are not only beautiful wooden chests but they also have inner cedar linings that protect linens, towels and even clothing for a long period of time."

"Can we also buy one for Tonia, Mama?" added Maria.

"That makes sense." Added Anna.

Prudence looked puzzled and her sister in law assured her that cash was not needed to buy the items. They could have them sent to the home COD, cash on delivery.

Weddings soon became a concrete reality. The two young future grooms went to visit Father O'Hern, pastor of St. Patrick's Church. The date was set for early the following fall. Lorenzo and Frank spent time looking for suitable living quarters. Apartments in a building adjacent to the hotel seemed good choices, at least until they decided to buy houses, suggested Lorenzo.

These two young girls were married at a simple wedding. True, the girls looked lovely in the beautiful dresses, designed and sewed by Maria. The wedding party was small, included only close family members and a few school friends of the boys and Tonia.

5
Living With Out Papers

Politicians and industrialists were quick to seize opportunities this city of Rochester was offering them. Many factories, buildings and homes were beginning to spring up in the city. Workers were needed. Immigrants and others looking for jobs became wage earners.

Lorenzo, too, was very much aware that he was headed for a future peppered with many prospects. When he returned from work, he would read business articles and often paused to read interesting bits to his wife. During these times Josephine became aware that her husband would not be content with a quiet uneventful life like his friends and countrymen. Always seeking new roads to travel, he confided in Josephine,

"We need to search for a home to purchase and I do want to expand my present work at the bank."

This young Italian girl, however, often felt alone and afraid. She longed for the company of her family. One day Prudence appeared offering to visit her daughter daily. If Josephine wouldn't mind, she would stop in to visit mornings after mass. The mother would stop to visit both her girls, especially since they were soon to be mothers. Life began to have a new spring in it for Prudence's daughters. Soon they too, accompanied their mother for morning Mass and contentedness began to dominate.

Oak and Smith Street area, the Tantalo's neighborhood, included immigrants from several countries. Although many spoke in foreign tongues, a climate of respect, caring and friendliness prevailed. Most of the non English-speaking residents were going to night school to learn the language that Americans spoke. Lorenzo urged Josephine to learn the language and take the test to become a citizen. Lorenzo had obtained his citizenship papers soon after his arrival in this foreign land. He was determined to receive his papers immediately. On his first day at the factory he heard one of the workers comment "What another Wop going to work here?" When he enquired as to the meaning of the statement he was told it meant WITH OUT PAPERS, therefore, were not citizens. Once he received his papers he would respond that he did have papers and was entitled to all the privileges of an American citizen. Many did not know what the derogatory word meant, were surprised and silenced.

Sophia, Josephine's cousin, came for a visit, noticed papers and an open dictionary on the kitchen table. When questioning her, the young bride explained,

"I'm studying English and am going to take a test to earn my citizenship papers."

"You are wasting your time, Pepina, It's much too soon for you to learn enough to pass the test," responded Sophia.

The proud young Italian was filled with joy when her papers did arrive.

As the strangeness of her new country began to wear off, Josephine became the smiling petite Italian newcomer of the block. Her neighbors on Oak Street, German immigrants and Irish immigrants living on Smith Street, began exchanging recipes from their own countries.

At the end of February, 1905 a golden haired brown-eyed girl was the first-born child of the Tantalos. This young couple planned a celebration for the Baptismal day of their little girl. Relatives and friends were invited but by the end of the day the couple as well as Prudence and Dominic were exhausted. Lorenzo assured his father in law,

"This is the first and last party we will have on the Baptismal day. The focus, as you pointed out a few days ago, Dominic, should be on the sacrament and the graces received. The group was rowdy and the men did have too much to drink." Filomena was the name of their first child. Both father and mother agreed it would be to honor of her absent grandmother.

"She will be educated to become a teacher like my mother and sisters," said Lorenzo the day they decided on the child's name. "Your mother was such a fine religious woman with many talents and I have so many beautiful memories of La Signor Filomena especially after my father left to come to America for a cure. Your mother helped me with my schooling and comforted all of us when we worried about our sick father. It would be a blessing if she did follow her example," added Josephine.

Other children followed in rapid succession and ultimately twelve children were born in this family but two boys did not survive. The second child died at infancy and the seventh was still born. The death of the second child took a heavy toll on Josephine those first years. The boy was eight months old, had a budding lively personality and when he suddenly fell ill with kidney problems, the memory of his pain took a long time to diminish. Another child, a girl was born soon after and diverted the young mother's attention to now another baby. Every two years a new child would become part of the growing family. Names were selected from the ancestral roster. Since all of Lorenzo's family was still in Italy, Josephine encouraged her husband to name the children after members of his family. All names were Italian names Annunciata, Pasqualina, Francisco, Antonia Mariucha, Dominic, followed by more English sounding names, Joseph, Ferdinand, Lucy and Amelia.

In the early nineteen hundreds, teachers did not hesitate to change a child's name if it was difficult to pronounce or was unfamiliar. Parental permission was never obtained. Changes were made in the first years of schooling and the Tantalo children were called, Frances, Nancy, Patricia, Francis, Mary, Dominic, Joseph, Fred, Lucy and Amy. Although Lorenzo strongly objected the name changes, he did not confront the teachers. He did, however make his point during report card time.

As each of the children presented a report card, the father scrutinized the report and after commenting on his pleasure or annoyance, depending on the marks, his attention would focus at the name on the card. His first gesture was to pick up a ruler, draw a line through the name written and then, above with his flourishing calligraphic hand, wrote the baptismal name of the child.

"They have written the wrong name on this card. Tell your teacher that she should correct her records "was the comment of the father. After several attempts, Lorenzo ignored the report card names and only focused on marks. Education and learning was important to the father with only good character and love of God taking priority.

Not long after the birth of the third child, the couple began searching for a suitable house to raise the children. A small house on the corner of Smith and Kent Streets was for sale. Discussing the need   to remain in the same neighborhood, Josephine expressed her wish to live in the little house on the corner. However, Lorenzo had already decided on their future home.

"That house does not have a cellar," her husband reminded Josephine. "It is not safe to live in a house that is not well built. Dampness and cold can bring on TB as well as rheumatism. There is a beautiful house on East Avenue that is going to be demolished to make room for one of the factory owner's mansion. It is affordable and George Kondolf is going to drive us there to examine it. He will be here this evening."

When Josephine was taken to examine the house she was overwhelmed at the size of the beautiful Victorian house. Although she was concerned at the size of this twelve-room structure, she knew her husband had already decided to make the purchase. In those days it was no major project to move houses from one street to another. Lorenzo purchased a tract of land along the canal. The parcel of land extended from Smith to Jay Streets and soon a cellar was dug on the corner of Oak and Smith Streets. This site where the cellar was dug became the resting place of the Tantalos' Victorian home. Real estate was available at an affordable price in Rochester at the beginning of the 20th century. Josephine knew other transactions were taking place. Businessmen appeared at their home and long conversations took up a good part of evenings.

Business activities began to decrease and Lorenzo invited Dominic and Prudence to have dinner with them. After the meal, the son-in-law told Josephine's parents he had purchased the hotel, which housed his bank exchange.

Dominic expressed his approval and congratulated the young man on his foresight.

"These are exciting times here in America today and it's well that you take advantage of opportunities that have promise."

It seemed a strange and unfamiliar business that Lorenzo was into and he often discussed happenings of the day with his wife. She worried about the long hours her husband remained at the hotel. The bulk of revenue came from the liquor and restaurant section of the enterprise. Hiring help became a problem because beer was the common beverage and the restaurant did not always serve meals that pleased customers of many different nationalities. Finally, two good bar tenders were employed and a husband and wife team ran the restaurant. Rent from small stores on the first floor was also a great source of profitable revenue.

Busy days followed with Josephine occupied with the children, running the large home and planning good meals for the family. Prudence often visited along with Maria and her children. Maria, too, was now living in the neighborhood, in fact not far from the corner and across from her sister's home. When the children gathered, they were instructed to remain on the large porch that surrounded the house. Gleeful sounds and happy shouts emanated from the group when barges or boats were seen gliding along the water. Days when his wife seemed overburdened, Lorenzo sent Graziella, the hotel housekeeper, to the house. Graziella was quick to help with tasks but proved too overpowering for Prudence and harsh with the children. Prudence explained to Lorenzo,

"The girls are young but it is important that they each have tasks around the house. They are good with the little ones and the house is much more peaceful without Graziella."

Two of the girls, Frances and Nancy were delighted to be free of the "bossy one." They took up tasks with enthusiasm when told that they no longer had Graziella helping. It became second nature to these lively growing children to take on additional little jobs as they continued to grow. Prudence was always quick to praise but patiently took time to correct faults with love. Josephine, the smiling gentle mother, too, was always ready to compliment them.

One evening in the mid year of 1919, Lorenzo's lawyer appeared at the Tantalo home. After greeting the couple, he was escorted to the parlor.

"Are you aware, Lorenzo, that soon you may not serve liquor at the hotel?" the visitor commented.

"Yes, I have been reading about the new law, National Prohibition of Alcohol, that will become law in 1920. I've been giving it much thought and have already begun to plan. The liquor stock is almost depleted and I shall be closing the taproom as well as restaurant before the end of the year. Tenants have been told that rooms will not be available after February. I am converting the hotel into apartments," answered the client.

"You are way ahead of me, Lorenzo, said the lawyer. "Please let me know if you need me," he said as he departed. Lorenzo assured him that he would be setting up a new business and would need his advice.

The couple then began discussing the possibilities after the lawyer left. Josephine told her husband she was happy with the change, never feeling comfortable about the hours spent at work. Lorenzo smiled and added,

"I do need to work, you know, but I'm converting the taproom and restaurant into a paint and wallpaper store and we will rent the apartments as soon as I've renovated the rooms. You are right, I'll be happy to give up the hotel business."

Many immigrants began asking for the apartments as soon as they realized the hotel would be converted. Paint and wallpaper salesman began to appear at Lorenzo's office, all anxious to be part of this renovation and ready to give advice. Lorenzo welcomed these salesmen and listened to them carefully. Many of these men advised the new businessman.

On one occasion, while discussing the progress he was making on the change over, Lorenzo commented,

"Salesmen have much to offer and should never be shortchanged. They know so much about the products they sell and how to display them. God is providing me with some wonderful advisors."

During the early 1920s, the Tantalos were well into a serene and comfortable routine. Friendly new neighbors were occupying apartments in the renovated building. Most of these new arrivals sought out their landlord for advice on work and other pertinent information. Work was not easily available. Foreigners encountered several obstacles. Most prevalent included unfamiliarity with the language and religious bias. Catholics were not hired at Kodak. Often the Irish met with signs at an employment site INNA (Irish need not apply). Most of the Irish immigrants were industrious and religious people.

George Eastman was getting to be a powerful man who was very selective and made no attempt to hide his dislike of religious people, especially Catholics. Soon Italians, too, were not being hired by the largest industry in Rochester. Many times, an immigrant seeking help after many tries to get employment would come to Lorenzo and ask for his help.

There were a number of smaller factories that did not hesitate to hire the newcomers. Realizing that they were hard working and willing employees, many of them became factory workers. A number of them did not find employment and had to be satisfied giving services to the rich on East Avenue. They became housekeepers, chauffeurs and cooks. Some men were hired only as what was referred to as Pick and Shovel Men. Although this was honorable work it took on a demeaning nature. Men with this manual work were paid very little and often were taunted by the crew's headman.

These were prosperous times in America. Industry was booming and many new exciting products were being manufactured. Among the most sought after items were cars, radios and electric fixtures. Homes were being converted from dim gas lighting to electricity. Lorenzo immediately sought out good electricians for the conversion from dim lights to the bright electric bulb. Since he was a reader, the change over became a necessity. Realizing how important reading was to her husband, Josephine encouraged her husband to change the lighting in their living quarters as well as the business. Often watching her husband squinting while reading, Josephine felt this new invention was needed.

Cars were beginning to move along the streets and soon many streets were being paved and converted from cobblestone to brick or tar. Lorenzo, too, soon purchased a model T Ford. Cars, horse drawn wagons and horse and buggies now shared roads. The horse and buggy was still very popular in the 1920s. Women felt comfortable driving a horse drawn carriage and were in awe of these new moving machines. Some were a little frightened, not used to the speed of the modern vehicles. Another drawback was that few of the common workingmen could afford a car.

Although the economy was at peak performance and Industrialists were making huge profits few could pay for the new inventions and items that were being displayed in the stores. Men of wealth were not purchasing but were investing in stocks. Some bought stocks on margin. The easy money of stock purchases would fascinate the inexperienced. When his friends boasted of the quick profit of stock purchases, Lorenzo would caution and advise them to be wary as money came only after hard work and careful investments.

Tenants that occupied the apartments would often try to save enough money to purchase their own house.

Immigrant's valued property especially houses with enough land for yards and vegetable gardens. Wages were low, unions were making little progress and families were large. Children needed food and clothing and parents prided themselves on providing well for their loved ones.

6
Homelessness, Alcoholics, Economic Depression

Pre depression times were happy times for immigrants living in the same neighborhood as the Tantalos. Children were well fed, cared for and loved. When children were not doing school assignments or home chores, they would hurry outdoors to play. Girls played hopscotch or jump rope and boys played baseball or creative games that involved balls or items for tossing about. Another favorite past time included jumping on the ice wagons to take chunks of ice. These were icebox days and ice was delivered by horse drawn wagons but the Tantalo children were not permitted to participate in this fun sport ever since Mrs. Miller snitched when she caught Frank and his cousin stealing the ice bits.

Inclement weather drove children indoors. Snow, however, was no problem. Sledding and skating were the great sports. Indoor games included marbles, checkers, jacks and other table games. The Tantalo girls, along with their friends and cousins liked sitting in the kitchen listening to stories of the Old Country. Mothers were great storytellers, often substituting listeners' names. It was during these listening sessions that children learned of their ancestors, their native land and struggles as well as accomplishments. During these get together times, Josephine's daughters liked to have their mother read old letters received from Italy. One that made a big impression was news of the 1915 earthquake. It was during that devastating time that children were told about Guiseppi, Lorenzo's youngest brother and pride of the family. Guiseppi and his wife were away for the day. The children were left home alone and the house was right in the path of the earthquake. Of course, the house was demolished and the children were killed. It was a terrible time for the couple. The shock had a drastic effect on the mother who was with child. Soon after childbirth, the mother and child died.

It was customary at that time that family members display by their apparel that a relative had died. Lorenzo immediately had a black armband made that was worn for a few months. The children observed and quietly spoke of the tragic event. A short time later a black edged letter arrived with additional sad news. It was the death notice of Lorenzo's father. Josephine urged her husband to leave for Italy and spend time with his family. Lorenzo assured Josephine that he would some day visit the family but would wait a while. His surviving brother and sisters were at home to help their mother with the sad changes in her life.

Death became a more concrete reality when Prudence's husband, Dominic, fell seriously ill. Josephine along with her brothers and sisters remained by the bedside praying softly while an occasional soft sob would be heard. Dominic died within a few days.

Deceased members of a family were waked at home. Front doors would be decorated with a large floral wreath, bright flowers if an adult had died or a smaller white wreath if it were a child. Passersby would pay their respects, be they acquaintances or not. Often children of different religions would also come into the front parlor where the body lay in state, knelt on the pew, said a prayer and quietly left the house.

Most families had an infant in the family and the Tantalo house was no exception. The children knew when there would be a new arrival. Grandma always came to stay for several weeks. Usually about a week after her arrival Dr.

Catamise would come with his black bag but before he went into their mother's bedroom he would line up the children and give each child a different colored pill. Soon the older children did not get in line as they realized pills were bits of candy. Before long a lusty cry would be heard, Lorenzo would appear in the living room and announced the gender of the new born. To the baby's cry loud cheers could be heard. The cheers came from the children of the same gender as the new baby.

Ever searching for additional property, Lorenzo purchased a twenty-acre track of land that included a large apple orchard and three houses. Additional real estate generated rental income. Prior to purchase and during the deliberating period, Prudence, as well as the older children, was included in the discussion. Francis, although only twelve years old, was listened to when asking questions.

"Papa, you said it is an apple orchard. Are there apples on the trees and if so who picks them up?"

"When the fruit is ripe, we can hire someone to hand pick the fruits. The cider mills will pick up what are left," answered the father.

The girls made no comment, Frank's older sisters realized it was a serious conversation and teasing would not be permitted at this time.

Patricia, usually shy, added, "Who will collect the rent?"

"Tenants will come to the store to pay rent or some of you can be shown how to ride on the bus to do the collecting," patiently responded the father.

"These children are fearless," thought Josephine somewhat in awe.

Soon after the last child was born, a rag factory was built several blocks from Lorenzo's home. He discussed the possibility of moving the family to the large house on the corner of Mount Reed Boulevard, a then rural section of

Rochester. It was on the recently acquired property. The home was large with a number of barns in the rear. The boys loved those barns and often invited their cousins and friends to spend weekends with them. Soon after the last child, Amy, started school, Josephine became lonesome for her friends and relatives in the old neighborhood. Lorenzo and Josephine discussed returning to Oak Street. The depression had just started and since the young people would have trouble finding work, Lorenzo thought unemployed family members could work in the store. It was not uncommon to see several of the children working in the store serving customers. It was at this time that the girls as well as the boys were trained to go to the bank, make deposits and also go to the newspaper offices where they inserted ads for rental property.

Many Rochester immigrants were without work. Some of the men worked as laborers in the WPA work project that was a government project started by President Roosevelt. It was a great blessing for the poor. A number of families lost their homes because they could not pay the mortgages. Many tenants, living in the rental homes owned by the Tantalos, lost their jobs. Lorenzo spoke to his wife of the many tenants that had lost work and were unable to pay rent. They decided it would not be good for them to evict these people from their homes as many landowners were doing. Tenants were told to remain in their homes until they found work. Many of them found work with the WPA and eventually they repaid the rent that was owed.

Another product of the depression was the number of homeless men. Many of them were jobless alcoholics. They paced along Main Street as well as State Street, the business section of Rochester. These men approached pedestrians. Begging for dimes and quarters. The lucky alcoholics would wend themselves toward Front Street and purchase drinks at the cheap saloons. Front Street fascinated the older Tantalo children. When going on errands that took them downtown, they would deliberately go to this section of the city. Front Street was peppered with saloons, cheap diners, chicken stores and small grocery stands.

Another section of town was also the gathering of these homeless men. A large empty factory on Lyell Avenue, which was referred to as McSweeny's Hotel, was converted into a homeless shelter. For very little, these men were given sleeping quarters. Since McSweeny's was not far from the paint store, men would stop in and ask for donations. Mr. Tantalo realized that many of these people were destitute because of the unemployment era. He sympathized with them and listened carefully to their requests. Very often he would offer them a meal and employment for the day. He would send word to his wife that he would not be home for lunch but to send sandwiches. He would be eating at the workplace. Josephine always knew what would transpire. Lorenzo confided when he first started the practice,

"There are many young men who can't find work and shame drives them to the streets. We must try to help them. But for the grace of God, I too would be among them."

"What can we do?" replied Josephine.

"Let's fix what used to be the hotel pool room into a small eating place. It is an empty storeroom now and we can easily find a table and a few chairs. They beg for food and money. I'll put them to work for a few hours, give them sandwiches with a small glass of wine. I'll give them only two dollars. It's not much but at least they will feel that they have a small job. If I send word, can you fix sandwiches for two?

I'll eat my lunch with them?"

"Of course, I'll be glad to help but do be careful just in case we may be too trusting," answered Josephine.

Lorenzo would often invite the worker to return another time if they wanted to work for just a short time. There were a few who did return occasionally. One man, John, came often. He was invited to learn how to wallpaper and paint homes. One of the customers hired him part time and finally John worked on his own. The Tantalo children listened attentively when their father related the outcome to his wife.

"Josephine, John is now working so that he can rent one of the apartments. Did you know he had a wife? She and their small son are living with the wife's parents. He wants to offer her a place to live so they can be family again. I'm going to offer the bottom floor of the house across the street. It is vacant now and we will not be getting much rent. We will not make much on the transaction but at least it will not be empty."

John or "John the Painter" as he was referred to, moved into his new home. Much to the dismay of the neighbors, John's wife was a cripple moving about with a wheelchair doing household chores and preparing meals with great dexterity. Neighbors often offered to help.

The depression era was met with great courage and patience by the immigrants especially those who did not speak English well. Some of the children would run into streets picking up bits of coal that fell from the coal trucks. Rochester had some cold winters and homes were heated with coal furnaces. Fuel was costly. Vacant lots also became sights that displayed real poverty. Many unemployed Italian men and women could be seen picking dandelions and other edible weeds. Often this was the main source of food. Women found a variety of ways to prepare these vegetables.

Families coped with this situation for several years.

New products were being put on the market and soon employment was available. Parents urged their children to become educated and many of them proved their worth by becoming dedicated workers no matter where work could be found. Not long into the recovery period there was talk of unrest in Europe. Lorenzo had already been planning to take his family to Italy for a visit. The children became aware of this when Frances called together the older children and gave them the information. She proved her point by opening a long drawer in the large dining room hutch. It contained new clothing for all the members of the family. There was great excitement at the prospect of travel. Travel plans, of course, had to be abandoned because of the turmoil in Europe.

Children of these courageous immigrants began to seize opportunities of many career options. As days quickly brought growth and change among the children of Josephine's household, this young mother remarked to Prudence one early summer day,

"Mama how fast these babies are getting to be young men and women. I'm losing control and Lorenzo is getting so impatient with them. They all have their own opinions that often differ from our way of thinking."

Prudence smiled, shook her head and replied, "Your children do not want to go the old paths. You , too, were stubborn. Remember, you did not want to continue your education and finally persuaded papa to your way of thinking. Your daughters do not want to be educators."

"After graduating from high school," Frances confided to her sister Nancy, "I will not attend the Normal School papa wants me to go to. I want to be a nurse and will ask to be admitted into a nursing school."

"You better be prepared for a flat refusal from papa. He was saying several weeks ago that he was sure you would follow our grandmother Tantalo's footsteps and ask to go to the Normal School," Nancy emphatically replied.

Nancy, the stubborn one, was waiting for a showdown. She, too, was determined not be get into the teaching profession. This would make her requests less shocking. Confronting day arrived too soon and Frances was not prepared for the alarming refusal. It was the usual Sunday evening when the older members of the family gathered in the two adjoining living rooms. Frances was explaining to her mother that she was applying for nurses training the next day. Lorenzo immediately asked,

"Where are you going tomorrow morning?"

"I'm not going to Normal School. I want to be a nurse," timidly replied Frances.

"Only if you want to be a doctor will I give my approval and pay for the education. Nurses are paid very little for their many services and risk getting contagious diseases."

Frances, Josephine and others listening to the conversation knew there would be no way Lorenzo would change his mind. Josephine, reminiscent of her own confrontations was overwhelmed. Her husband was not as easy to be persuaded as her father was. Nancy prepared for the outcome, motioned Frances to follow. Both girls left the room and went upstairs to the girls' quarters. There Nancy gave her sisterly advice.

"Don't give in, Frances, just do not go to school at all in the fall. You know how papa is about our getting a good education. Go and find a job and don't wait until September. He will not even notice that you are not home daytimes. He is too busy at the store."

Surprisingly, Frances did get work immediately at a radio sound equipment industry. There was a vacancy in the engineering room for a math calculator. Since she did have good math skills, Frances was immediately hired. She was to report for work the following Monday. Frances shared the news on arriving home at lunchtime. Josephine was not alone. Aunt Maria and Prudence were visiting. Nancy and Patricia were also in the kitchen when Frances enthusiastically explained her job experimenting with florescent lighting and radio equipment.

"How much will they be paying you and how many hours a week will you be working?" inquired Aunt Maria.

The three adult women discussed the situation at length while the young girls waited expectantly. Finally it was Prudence who silenced them all. She would approach Lorenzo and relay the news giving him many reasons why he should give this young girl permission to work. Lorenzo always valued the advice of his mother-in-law. He quickly realized that he was no expert on American women in the workplace. His business associates often spoke of their daughters, wives and the new women's movements.

"Lorenzo, give your daughter Frances time at the work place. She is young and may change her mind later," Prudence advised on the Sunday afternoon when the subject came up and the girls had left to go to the movies.

With a visible display of disappointment, the father shrugged his shoulders and nodded to Josephine, "she has already given her word, better let her go," added the father. The subject was immediately dropped as the women realized how difficult it was for the father's admission of defeat.

Life became much less burdensome for Josephine. Her daughters began sharing many more of the household tasks and responsibilities. It was customary to refer to the newborn as Baby. The previous baby was referred to as Big Baby. The eldest child always took charge of the BIG BABY while the mother cared for the new infant. When Frances started working, it delighted Nancy. She would now be in charge of the older of the two youngest ones. Mary was the

Big Baby when Nancy took up the task. Mary often recalled how painful it was when she was no longer young enough to have a baby sitter. It was Dominic that was now the Big Baby. He would receive all Nancy's attention. When she returned from school, Nancy and her friends would take the young ones out for a stroll around the neighborhood. Often these girls would pass the ice-cream store and share Ice cream with the little occupants of strollers. Mary missed the laughter and treats, however, she soon discovered playmates. There were young children everywhere. Children comfortably visited each other's homes frequently being invited to remain for a meal. Of course, these young ones were trained to first inform their mothers of the invitations and asked permission to dine with friends.

There was a growing closeness among the neighbors, relatives and school friends of this section of Rochester. A neighbor's illness was everyone's business. Housewives fixed meals, delivered them and spent time with the sick.

While children were in school, mothers kept busy with home tasks, taking care of babies and weather permitting, would sit on their porches, chatting with neighbor as they breast-fed a child. Breast-feeding was a common practice. One of the neighbors, having lost her husband while she was with child, found work at a clothing factory soon after the baby was born. The grandmother took up the responsibility of caring for the children during the daytime. On school days, the oldest child would pick up the infant during her lunchtime and meet the mother at a small park near the factory. The mother would breast-feed the baby. Mother and daughter went without lunch on those days.

As children matured, grew old enough to attend high schools they began exploring other neighborhoods. Schoolmates invited them to visit their homes. They found some similarities. All neighborhoods had their own national churches be they Protestant or Catholic. Most of the Jewish synagogues were on the East side. The Oak and Smith Street neighborhood was on the West Side. Rochester had the Gennessee River flowing in the center of town. This was a natural division. Residents of the city began referring to the sides of the city as the west and the east sides. These high school years had great influence on the young. Among the greatest impact included life long friends.

7
Clash of Cultures, Zoning,
Teaching Integrity in the Workplace

Young people attending high schools during the early twentieth century had no input on subjects they would be taking. It was standard procedure to classify incoming students and assign them to either an academic or commercial program.

When Nancy was ready for high school she decided to change over to a public school.

"I'm not going to a Catholic school in the fall, Pat, I want to take subjects that I choose."

"That's a good idea, I think I'll do the same thing when it's my turn to go to high school," agreed Patricia, the loyal follower of her sister.

Refusal from her father did not deter this stubborn daughter. She went silently about house tasks as well as store responsibilities. Josephine intervened and Nancy was allowed to select the school of her choice. However, a sad awaking took place. The school she selected did not give her choices either. The same as the academy, Nancy was again placed in an academic program.

"Pat, can you believe it? I must take all the subjects that are assigned to me. The schedule includes Latin and no art. I wanted art."

"What are you going to do now?" questioned Patricia.

"Well, there are boys in all my classes. I like that" added Nancy, with a triumphant look.

Young people were enthusiastic, and energetic always ready to embark on unfamiliar fields. All too soon and much to the concern of her mother, Nancy completed high school and decisions had to be made. No, Nancy would not be going to normal school but decided to take courses in dress design. She met no opposition. Lorenzo was a very busy man and thought it might be a worthy path for her to take. This enterprising young woman immediately found employment despite the unemployment problem. O'Hare, an exclusive hat designer, hired her. Women of means wore custom made hats that matched the outfits they wore.

Patricia, however, did not achieve her desire to become an artist. This shy daughter of Josephine and Lorenzo managed to take art courses in high school. One of her instructors, recognizing her talents, suggested Patricia go to an art college in New York City. Of course, she met with great opposition.

"My art teacher, Mr. Taylor, is coming to speak to papa. He suggested I continue studying art in New York. I would like that," confided Pat to her sister Nancy.

"Forget it! You don't want to go to New York. In fact, Papa and even Mama will refuse to let you go," replied the alarmed older sister.

One early evening, several days later Mr. Taylor appeared at the paint store. He was ushered into the office and Patricia was summoned to hear the request.

"Your daughter is a talented art student. May I suggest Patricia be sent to a fine art school in New York City. She will not only be accepted but is also eligible for an art scholarship."

Lorenzo responded almost harshly, "An art career is out of the question. Artists need a powerful patron and as a women artist, she would have few job opportunities."

Patricia left the office immediately and found Nancy nearby listening to the conversation. The two went to the upstairs girls' quarters. There, Pat burst into tears.

"Don't get upset, it isn't the end of the world. You can come and work with me. I'll teach you," comforted Nancy.

"I hate hats and I don't like that kind of work," Pat replied.

Frances, returning from work walked into the study area toward their rooms and wanted to know what all the fuss was about. When Pat, between sobs, recounted the day's happenings, Frances, after reflecting, added,

"You don't have to decide right away. You haven't even graduated yet. You are very young. Remember, you skipped several classes when you were in grammar school. That is going to make you still an adolescent when you graduate.

I wouldn't send a child to New York if I were a parent. We don't have relatives in New York City. Just wait a year after you graduate. You may find opportunities right here in Rochester," Frances reassured her young sister.

The conversation was immediately stopped as the girls heard Josephine mount the stairs.

"Pat, papa told me about the school in New York. I would miss you so much if you went away. You are still my little girl and so helpful to me," pleaded the mother.

"Mama, Pat is going to wait a while after graduating. She may attend a Rochester school instead," immediately spoke up Nancy to halt the mother from worrying. Visibly relieved, the mother looked around and continued, "Why don't we all go downstairs and visit with grandma, she just came in for a short visit."

"Large families offer opportunities for quick relief from troublesome situations," thought Josephine as she softly whispered a short prayer of thanksgiving.

Francis, now a high school student, was spending more time in the store as Lorenzo began teaching him some of the techniques used to purchase stock. Often, Mary and Dominic also silently stood by. On one occasion, the three children were taught a lesson that was never forgotten. A large load of wallpaper was delivered to the store. The job of stocking always fell to the boys. Rolls of paper were unrolled and as the texture and pattern were examined, Lorenzo would quote a price to be marked on the bin that held like stock. On that particular day, high quality stock was being examined.

"Frank, you guess the price I will quote" encouraged the father.

Lorenzo would listen, repeat the price quoted and then lowered the prices considerably.

"Why do you charge so little, papa" the offended boy remarked. "I have been spending time visiting other paper and paint stores. I saw like paper and it was priced much higher than you are giving to the same stock," continued Francis.

"Remember what I now tell you. First you take into account the cost of the merchandise. Then consider not only the value of the stock but the customers you will be serving. Most of our customers are poor. They work hard for their pay. This load was a bargain for us and it is wrong to make too large a profit when a poor person needs the product. We are making a good living, not taking advantage of those that are more unfortunate than we are. God's blessings will be upon our work when we show compassion."

Dominic and Frank often repeated the same words to the younger brothers, Joseph and Fred when they, too, were learning to price. Lorenzo's words of integrity at the work place made a lasting impression on the two older boys.

There were other occasions when the father pointed out the difference between right from wrong.

On one particular Friday evening Francis, Dominic and their two cousins were sitting on the front steps of the store, laughing heartily and pointing to someone. Glancing out the front door, Lorenzo noticed that the cousins' father was tottering as he walked towards the young men. No doubt but that Maria's husband had spent some of his Friday's wages at the saloon before going home.

Lorenzo immediately and firmly ordered all of the boys to come into the store. He sternly looked at them silently for a short time then spoke seriously while pointing to the two cousins,

"That was your father. He goes to work each day so that you can be well fed, have warm clothing and good food to eat. Your father hates his job. It is not easy to dig with pick and shovel outdoors on very cold and very hot days. Remember, he had a good job in Italy. He is intelligent, not educated and can't speak English. Your father drinks to make him forget. He needs help and that must come from his children. Show him that you appreciate what he does for you."

Another lesson on right and wrong took place on a summer Saturday afternoon. Again, the two cousins along with Francis and Dominic went riding along with Lorenzo to collect rent. Finally the car stopped at the last house on the list of tenants. When Lorenzo stepped out of the car Mr. and Mrs. Johnson, the occupants of the house, approached him, they led the landlord to a garage that was in need of repair. While the adults were discussing repairs, the boys left the car and wandered to the rear of the house. On seeing an open trap door leading to the cellar, the boys laughingly went into the basement and noticed canned fruit jars resting on shelves in a storage area. Dominic picked a jar of fruit and leading the others rushed into the car and deposited the bottle of pears in the back seat, hiding it from view. The boys laughingly awaited the return of Lorenzo. On driving off, the boys were unusually quiet and then sudden bursts of giggles would be heard. After

58

the second outburst, Lorenzo stopped the car and looked into the back seat. He observed the jar, immediately returned to the driver's seat, turned around speeding toward the Johnson's home. On arrival, he ordered the boys to pick up the jar of fruit, go to the tenants, explain their theft and ask for a chore to be done.

Of course, Mrs. Johnson would not hear of a chore, offered them the fruit and accepted the apology. Lorenzo remained in the car and the boys did not take the jar with them on their return. It was a silent and tense ride back to Oak Street. On hearing of the account, Josephine was astounded and replied, "Why did they steal fruit? They will seldom eat pears that are served at the table."

Josephine, too, had a way of letting the children know right from wrong. A more subtle way was selected. Sunday mornings children often spent mornings in the kitchen while dinner was being prepared. The mother would repeat the Sunday Gospel but recounted it in a story form that interested the young audience. She often gave examples of following the teachings in their lives. Josephine did not limit Gospel teachings to children alone. On one occasion this frail woman firmly redirected her husband.

"I need to run an errand. Can you answer the phone while I am away? Calls should be coming in answer to this morning's newspaper ad. One of the houses on Avery Street is vacant. I'd like a quick rental and it would be helpful if you get all the information necessary," requested Lorenzo.

The answer was prompt and enthusiastic. "I'll bring my sewing basket and am happy to sit down and do some mending while I wait for calls."

On her husband's return, Lorenzo's petite wife beamingly showered him with the good news.

"The house is rented, Lorenzo. A lovely family phoned and after my approval came to make a deposit. They will come again late this afternoon to sign the agreement."

Before long Josephine heard a lengthy discussion in the office and recognized voices of the new tenants. Her husband left the group and came into the adjoining room to talk to his wife.

"The new tenants are black and they have four children. Avery Street is in a restricted zoned area. Families moving in must meet the designated requirements. Inhabitants in that area have few children and are white folks."

"These are people that need a home to live in and I don't understand the reasoning at all. You get in touch with your lawyer and get this wrong righted. It's an inhuman request and it is very wicked." With that statement, Josephine left the office area and went into the kitchen. She took up a broom and immediately began to sweep the floor that was clean. She vented her anger not in words but work.

"Josephine is right. It is a heartless law," thought the father of ten children. He returned to the couple and after they signed the agreement, Lorenzo called his lawyer and let him handle the zoning board. He smiled after the phone call to the attorney and discovered his lawyer was easier to handle than his wife.

Sundays were special days especially in the Tantalo family. It was a day that all went to church. As the children became older they selected the time they would be attending Mass. Friends often returned home with them and were invited for Sunday dinner. Their Uncle Lazarus attended the last Mass and on the way home he too would stop in for a visit.

Josephine's brother would enter by the front entrance and immediately begin playing popular songs on the grand piano in the living room. All the young people would gather around him, sing along, laugh and tease. Pat Costa, a friend of

Nancy, would also be in the group of young people. She had a lovely voice and often the others would stop singing.

They just listened to this young soprano. Lazarus would rise, give the piano bench to Pat and go into the kitchen for a brief visit with his sister.

Pat Costa was not only a friend of Nancy's but soon the two sisters, Frances and Patricia also became the singer's friend. Children from both families exchanged home visits. Other Costa children with like interests and ages, became life long friends also. Among the most frequent exchange visits included short stays by Jenny and Anna. Within a few years, Mary and Antoinette also became friends.

During one of the visits, the Costa girls persuaded their mother to meet Mrs. Tantalo. The two women had like leanings. These mothers found much to talk about. The Costas lived on the East side of Rochester. Their near neighbors were Polish, Jewish, Germans and Italians. Germans and Italians living on the East side, however came from different sections of their native lands.

During one of these visits, Mrs. Lena Costa confided,

"I don't go to church, Josephine. My Catholic religion is important to me but the last time I attended Mass was fifteen years ago. After my marriage, my husband found employment in the Pennsylvania coal mines. It was a terrible experience. My husband worked incredibly hard in the damp coal mines with modest pay. Money purchased very little because the mine manager also owned the general store. The pastor of the church did not help us. In fact, he charged to baptize a child. When my third child was born, we didn't have enough money. The priest refused to baptize the baby and told us to return when we had the fee. We never returned to the church again."

With profound sorrow, Josephine empathized, "What a terrible experience. Even priests, like the rest of us, can be self serving and greedy. Since all my experiences with churchmen have been good, I don't know how I would act if that happened to me. Lena, our men are proud and demanding. It is difficult to try finding excuses for such behavior. All you can do is pray and I, too, will offer prayers."

It disturbed Josephine even more when she discovered that some of the Costa children were non-believers and espoused the Communist Atheistic philosophy. Josephine, however, was greatly relieved when the Costa children became Saturday overnight guests and went to Mass with the Tantalo girls. A certain amount of anxiety remained with the mother as the friendships also included the Costa boys.

Frances often brought up the subject of communism when all the friends gathered in the upstairs rooms. These young people were constantly reading literature related to the subject. Each member of the group tried to persuade the other side. Over and over again the word PROPAGANDA came up. When the conversation became too intense, Patricia Tantalo would change to some fun stuff. Their fun and stay at home entertainment included listening to music records, listening to Nancy recite comic poetry or discussing the latest famous movie stars. They paired a star with one of the group. Nancy would be compared to Norma Shearer, Frances to Mary Pickford, Patricia to Claudette Colbert while Anna a Gloria Swanson Jenny was a Mary Brian and Pat Costa resembled Loretta Young.

"Let's check the new movie magazines," and thus Patricia would introduce the look a like subject.

The Serafine cousins, Lucy and Mae would habitually join this group of young women. When smoking became a fad with movie stars, these young girls would buy a pack of cigarettes and try   smoking in imitation of the actresses. Lucy normally absented herself from the group, fearing the Tantalo parents would catch them.

62

"Why worry, Lucy," would comment her sister Mae. "This is a private place. You know that Uncle and Aunt never come up here and it is out of bounds for the boys."

Dating, another subject, often was discussed and debated during the get together. Neighbors and brothers were never included when the girls went on dates. Normally the girls would double date or attend a function with several couples. Fathers and brothers were always ready to pass judgment on the selections of their male companions. When an affair required formal attire the girls came into the parlor to greet their escorts who were in tuxedos. The boys of the family would also present themselves with wide grins.

"When the girls have company do not interfere. It is rude and very unbecoming." Reproved Josephine.

The girls' brothers soon stopped the teasing. They left their taunts for the next day. Scrutiny by fathers, brothers and even close friends saved many of the young women from impulsive dating. Frances and Anna, the eldest of the group, were quick to identify high risk male companions. Following would be some of the questions that their big sisters asked them. Questioning usually followed if one of the girls dated the same fellow several times without the company of other couples.

"Do you admire him enough to introduce him to Papa, Mama and even our aunts and uncles?"

"Do you know your friend's family and does he introduce you to his parents"

"Where did you spend the evening?"

These barrages of questions were a great deterrent for dangerous flirtations.

Friends and even family members, however, were quick to give approval if they felt the young man was a worthy escort. Even salient virtues were revealed.

8
Teenage Conflicts, Career Choices, Public Schools

Neighborhood transformations were rapidly taking place on Oak and Smith Streets. Young men and women were fast making their marks. Children were still in the majority but many of the mothers seemed to have more time to visit, go to daily Mass and exchange bits of gossip.

Frequently when her girls enjoyed their mother's company, while the younger were at play, some surprising information was exchanged. Most of the bits of gossip were revealed to Josephine by one of her girls.

"Where did you hear that strange gossip?" Josephine would ask the informant.

Usually, the news would be overheard while the girls visited neighbors or relatives. Targeted families included the Bello family or the Franciscos. Both families were new to the neighborhood. Mr. And Mrs. Bello and five children, ranging in age from ten to nineteen, made up tenants that moved into the top floor of the Victorian home across from the paint store. A much more mysterious family purchased the large Miller home and were considered to be snobbish by the young men and women in the neighborhood.

"Mama, Antoinette lives next door to the Franciscos and she said that shortly after they moved in, policemen appeared at their home. Earsplitting shrieks were heard before the police arrived. The oldest daughter had just returned from their honeymoon and a few days later a quiet private funeral was held. The son-in-law is now in jail and Antoinette thinks her husband murdered the new bride. Isn't that awful?" the wide-eyed horrified Patricia recounted.

"Yes, mama," added Nancy, "I heard the story, too."

"My dears, that is terrible gossip to be spreading. Don't destroy reputations by dreadful gossip,"

Different versions of the tragedy were recounted over the years and Frances agreed with her mother and attributed it to jealousy. She became friendly with Grace Francisco, a classmate who often invited her to attend concerts at the Eastman Theatre. Grace, however, never accepted invitations to visit any of the nearby neighbors. Mrs. Francisco was aloof and unfriendly answering greetings with a brief nod and a non-smiling expression. Unlike most immigrants, they were not churchgoers. One of the Protestant girls, living on Smith Street, admitted the family once did attend the Lake Avenue Baptist church when they first moved into the neighborhood.

James, however, a handsome bright boy, quickly became friends with the neighborhood group participating in their games and sports. Jim was a few years older than Francis but they often went to the library together. Both boys liked to read and always returned to their homes with several books. This young fellow visited the Tantalo family often.

When he attended the university in Rochester, he invited Patricia to go to the movies with him or attend a school function. Patricia always refused and it troubled Josephine. Convinced that the malicious gossip had destroyed the boy's family reputation. She felt sure her daughter was aloof and fearful because of the scandal.

"How dreadful that sinful tales are ruining the reputation of those fine children," added the girls' mother when she listened to her daughters Nancy and Pat discussing the invitations and her daughter's refusals.

"Mama, that is not the reason for the refusals. I just get bored with his company and he is very boastful," Patricia assured her mother.

Unlike the Franciscos, the Bello family was pitied and became the concern of both the young as well as the adults. Shortly after this new family moved into their new home, Dominic enquired,

"Mama, why doesn't Vincent Bello go to work? He's nineteen years old and spends most of the day wrapped in a blanket and sitting on the front porch."

"That family is experiencing some troubled times. The eldest daughter died just before they moved across the street. Tuberculosis took the first child and it seems that the boy, too, is very sick. We need to pray for them. You can help the family by inviting the younger boys to join you at play. Remember to be kind," replied the mother sadly.

A life long friendship developed between Dom and Angelo Bello as a result of the conversation between mother and son. The two boys attended the same schools and the youngest Bello son, Sam, was often beckoned by Dominic to accompany them when they went to the movies.

The youngsters treasured Saturdays. This was their day for fun and play. If the weather was pleasant, streets and sidewalks became their playground. Girls played jump rope or hopscotch. Boys played ball, tag and at times taunted the girls by interrupting their play. Catholic boys and girls went to Confession on Saturdays. Mothers usually stepped out on the front porch shouting,

"It's time to go to Confession." After a few grumbles, children left their play and wended their way to St. Patrick's Church. All the young went be they Catholics, Protestants or Jewish. Girls tried to arrive before the boys. Many of the boys remained in the Confessionals longer. Father Mooney usually gave them a tailor made lecture. Father O'Brien was a young curate and gave lighter penances.

There were occasions when the boys became unruly running up and down the aisles laughing and giggling. Father Mooney would step out of the Confessional, order them to leave the church and return in a silent line seating themselves singly and silently. When the boys were reprimanded, the girls were sure to go home and tell on them. The boys would inflict a few days of silent treatment on the girls.

"You're a bunch of snitches," the boys would sneer.

One early summer drizzly afternoon a tragic event dismayed the neighborhood. Jerry, the Cooney boy, went swimming several streets away where the canal was treacherous on rainy days. Mr. Cooney, on his way from work noticed a large crowd gathered along the bank of the canal. Firemen and police were in a boat and loud gasps and crying drew the father to the group. It was his son, Jerry. Mr. Murphy, the policeman, was holding the boy's naked body. The body was turning blue while being lifted out of the waters. Tearfully, the father came forward, took his son and carried him home with sobs. He was inconsolable walking towards his home with his precious son.

Within a few days a flower wreath was displayed on the front entrance door of the Cooney home. Two viewing days brought droves of neighbors and their children to the home. Children knelt, prayed briefly and departed silently. Mothers, however, sat for long hours with the family and the men gathered at the Cooney home evenings. Jerry's drowning was the topic of conversation for a long time. Fathers' often referred to the event when cautioning their children about the dangers of swimming in restricted waters. Irondequoit bay, another treacherous swimming place, was a definite no no for the Tantalo children.

Young adults spent Saturdays and Sundays visiting friends, attending movies and if fortunate went out on dates.

Frequently when Pat Costa spent the weekend with the Tantalos, Nancy and Patricia would accompany Pat to her home. One of the Costa boys would drive the girls back to Oak Street.

Usually the girls arrived at the Costa home on the East side of town early Sunday afternoon. Lively conversations were interspersed with bouts of music sessions. Neighbors and friends of the Costas also joined the group. Among the most popular topics included labor unions and politics. Patricia was somewhat uncomfortable with some of the topics but Nancy was very vocal. If Frances joined her sisters, she took the unpopular stance. She disagreed with organizing employees and especially spoke against CLOSED SHOP.

"I don't want some union leader telling me what I should do or how I should act. If I don't like my work environment, I'll just quit and find another job," heatedly replied Frances.

"It's fine for you to quit your job. You are not the father of a large family or need to help support a wife and children with meager wages. We went through hell at the mines. I was just a boy, had to help the family and didn't even go to high school. The mines were dark, damp and cold. Our days were long and wages purchased very little," just as heatedly responded Lenny.

Gilda, a lovely red headed Jewish girl and near neighbor of the Costas, dear friend of Nancy and Pat Costa, always sided in with Nancy and Frances. She, too, animatedly expressed her views.

"Lenny, you know that some of the leaders of Unions are unscrupulous and don't hesitate to put their mitts into the till robbing the organization's dues. They can incite crowds into violent acts. Many times strikes erupt into demonstrations.

Such was the case during the Haymarket Riot," screeched Gilda, waving her arms to emphasize her point of view.

Anna would follow with her contributions. This new bride, married to a firm believer in strikes, was quick to take up causes related to labor disputes.

"Let me remind you, Gilda, that not so long ago the poor were working as much as eighty hours a week with very little pay. Children were part of the work force, too. It was the unions that obtained many of the privileges you enjoy now. It has been a hard struggle, bosses are always ready to fire at the least provocation and quick to revoke the privileges won with years of tough bargaining.

Frequently, these lively discussions would be interrupted. Lenny with a beaming expression would pick up his mandolin and burst into song. Lenny was a handsome fellow, tall with dark wavy hair and a beautiful smile which lighted up his whole face. These spurts of song habitually took place when the gentle Mrs. Costa walked into the room.

All would join in the singing while a few would leave for the kitchen where they helped set places in the dining area. Soon food would be served and lighter chatter would follow. Departures were never too late. Many of the young had factory jobs. Morning came all too quickly and work was demanding. Jobs were swiftly lost. Unemployment checks were not issued during that time.

During the ride back to Oak Street Patricia would sit in the back seat with Frances and Pat Costa. Nancy usually sat with the driver, Lenny. After they arrived home and were settled in the upstairs rooms, Pat would report her observations, "Nancy, Lenny is so handsome and he often glanced your way especially while he was singing love songs. He's in love with you. Why don't you go steady with him?" With great impatience Nancy habitually would answer,

"He is an atheist and communist you know."

"He is not a communist, Nancy," would respond Frances. "The Costas are Communist sympathizer."

"Same thing," and with the final say, Nancy would leave the company and reflect on her own feelings. It was difficult to admit to herself that she really was very fond of her friend's brother. She would not give up her church's teachings. A believer with unwavering faith, Nancy could make choices that did not compromise her values. Her friend Pat Costa was aware of her dear friend's dilemma. Many times these two friends discussed religion, marriage, careers including struggles and temptations. Both agreed that it was better to resist as soon as temptations came along.

"Better be safe than sorry." They would assert at the end of their long ponderings.

The group of young women that met on the top floor of the Tantalos' home occasionally included the younger girls. The older girls dominated much of the conversation but on occasion the young were listened to. The big sisters were generous in complimenting the youngsters. These younger members were anxious to be accepted and listened carefully to conversations. They were quick to imitate their models. Many wise words were exchanged.

Francis and Mary both attended the same public high school and they often supported each other when conflicts arose. Soccer was considered too violent for Mr. Tantalo and he did not allow his boys to go to the games. When after school games were being played, Frank persuaded his younger sister to find an excuse to remain in school after hours. Francis implied Mary needed a ride home and, therefore, remained after school to accommodate his sister.

A touring car was purchased to accommodate several family members. The Ford was a smaller car and it was transferred to Francis. Of course, he had to spend Saturdays making paint and wallpaper deliveries. High school students considered it a privilege to drive to school.

One early morning, after picking up several of his friends, Francis and the boys drove by the orchard. This was a twenty-acre apple orchard. It was late in the season, over ripe bad apples remained on the ground.

"Let's pick up some of the rotten fruit and take them to school. We can have some fun," said one of the students.

An empty basket was filled to overflowing. It was still early when the boys arrived at the back parking lot. Within minutes, a tossing of soft apples ensued. Dodging, laughter and loud whoops could be heard. A crowd of students gathered. Splashing, sliding and yells continued for a few minutes. Noticing a teacher was observing, the group quickly dispersed leaving a slushy mess at one end of the parking lot.

Francis knew that he was in trouble. He immediately sought out his younger sister Mary and told her to admit nothing if she was called to the office. As soon as she arrived in her homeroom, Mary was summoned out of the room by one of the teachers and told to report to the principal's office.

"Mary, I understand that your family has a large apple orchard. Did Francis drive to school this morning?" asked Mr. Jenner.

"I left home before my brother," Mary timidly and softly responded.

"Does your brother always drive to school?'" was the next question.

"I'm not sure," was the reply.

"These students will not divulge anything," thought the principal.

He dismissed the students that were being questioned and picked up the phone. The dreadful truth occurred to all of them. Mr. Tantalo would be receiving a phone call.

"Did your son drive to school this morning?" said the principal after a very short greeting.

"He always takes the car to school" responded Lorenzo. He immediately thought that Frank was in an accident.

After the principal told Lorenzo of the involvement of his son, he assured him that no great damage had been done. It could be quickly remedied. Mr. Jenner did admit to Lorenzo that both his children were not only good students but their conduct had also been faultless in the past.

While the students were waiting in the outer office they decided they would admit what they did and the role of each of the group. It didn't take long for the culprits to clean the mess.

Frank drove Mary home from school both knowing that it was better to get their punishment immediately rather than spend time guessing what would take place. All of the guilty students would have to remain indoors during lunch periods for a month. That was the punishment the involved students received from the principal

"You lied to the principal, Mary, that is unforgivable," was the first statement from the father. "You will not be driving to school for a month, Frank," ordered Lorenzo to his son. Both young people went to their rooms and silence predominated the supper table that evening. Both guilty participants were grateful that the father would be working late and not be present during the meal. He would eat later and discuss the matter with his wife.

These two Tantalo children enjoyed their time spent at this suburban high school. Marshall High was close to Sacred Heart, a Catholic Church. During lunchtime many of the Catholic students went to the church for short visits. Lunch hour was almost an hour long and teachers, too, could be seen going in and out of the church. It was a public school that encouraged students to attend worship services of all denominations. Announcements came over the address system reminding the students of holy days and worship services. Latin was used at all the Masses during this time. One of the Latin teachers encouraged Catholic students to bring their Missals to school Fridays. He would go over the Mass and translations were exchanged thus giving a better understanding of Sunday's gospel readings.

Mary was new to Marshall High School. Her first choice after graduation from grammar school had been Nazareth Academy. Late August, Mary became ill and it resulted in missing the first three weeks of school. Her friends, all attending Nazareth, assured Mary that school was rigid with strict rules and lots of homework.

"You will never get caught up with us when you return to school," Julia and Virginia assured Mary, her two close friends. After consulting with her brother Frank, she decided to go to the public high school. Frank attended Marshall High. "Why don't you come to my school? You will like the teachers and students. I can drive you to school most of the time." With that assurance, Mary decided that she would attend the public school.

Although Mary liked public grammar school there were several problems she encountered at the junior high level. Both math and English teachers were excellent. History, one of Mary's favorite subjects, was taught by Mrs. Croft, a lazy teacher that gave no presentations, children read silently and answered end of chapter questions. This led to a habitual bad practice on Mary's part. She would often bring a library book to class, hide it over the textbook and would read novels during class time. She had read the history book over and over again and boredom predominated the whole period unless she read one of her library books.

Mrs. Croft reported the pastime to the principal who in turn phoned Mr. Tantalo and passed the information to the girl's father. This resulted in months without the child going to the neighboring library to borrow books.

"The principal called me today and said Mary is reading novels during history period instead of doing the assigned work given by the instructor. She is not to borrow books from the library until the end of the term. Check to make sure she has only school books when she returns home," Lorenzo told his wife.

There were times when Mary did go to the library after school but sneaked the books into the house. One of the younger children was instructed to be near the parlor at a certain time late afternoon and signal the whereabouts of her mother. Window shades in front of the house were raised or lowered to certain levels depending on where the mother was. If Josephine was in the living room the shade would remain at the usual level and Mary would hide the library books behind the cellar trap door. If Josephine was in the kitchen, which was her usual place, Mary would remove her shoes and quickly mount the stairs and bring her treasure to her bedroom.

A more serious event that had the full sympathy of her parents took place during gym class. Miss Johnson was a short stocky gym teacher who didn't hesitate to use her fists.

Boys and girls had exercise classes at the same time.

She took an instant dislike to Eugene, an eighth grader that was several inches taller than Miss Johnson. This boy could become very surly, however he did respond to kindness and good teaching. All the Beulers were good students and Eugene was no exception. Miss Smith, the math teacher, often gave this boy her car keys and would instruct him to get material from the trunk of her car. He was proud of the chore and was one of the top math students.

Eugene did not fare so well with the gym teacher. On one occasion, Miss Johnson repeatedly corrected him for very minor infractions. He mumbled under his breath and before the end of the period, she stood directly in front of him

Daring him to repeat an obscenity. When he did so, she slapped him in the face and he in turn shoved the teacher and stamped out of the gymnasium.

The boy went home and as a result was expelled from school. No action was taken to reinstate him or find another school for the boy. With time on his hands, he joined a group of young men that were being sought out for their role in several robberies. Eugene became one of their look out men. During a confrontation with the police and detectives, Eugene was fatally shot by accident.

Some very painful days followed this event. The Beulers were devastated. Two of his younger sisters were inconsolable.

"That is one of the saddest wakes I have ever attended," Josephine confided to her daughters."

The Beuler family moved out of the neighborhood and very few knew of their whereabouts. The event made quite an impression on Mary. She did not like to think of the episode. She had often walked to school with the Beuler girls and was happy she did not have to return to that school in the fall.

It was one of the deciding factors that gave direction to the choice of schools. This child wanted to attend a Catholic

School. Illness and comments of Julia and Virginia, however, made her choose Marshall.

"Do you think I should transfer to a Catholic school?" Mary asked after the apple tossing incident. "I have been at Marshall just a little over a month and am already in trouble," continued the younger sister.

"Don't be foolish, boys always get in trouble and since Frank is graduating and you already have some very nice friends. Stay there for at least the rest of the school year," advised her big sister. Mary acted on Pat's advice and became more aware of potential friends. The younger girl admired her older sisters and always sought their approval. She was especially fond of her sister Pat. Pat was serious, intelligent and pretty.

Many times when the   two were alone in the upstairs rooms before Frances and Nancy returned from work, Pat and Mary would have chats and exchange dreams of the future. Mary was quick to remind Pat that she was the prettiest girl in the neighborhood with big beautiful light brown eyes, high cheekbones, flawless skin and pearly teeth. Pat in turn would tell Mary that she would prefer the color of Mary's hair. The older sister knew that Mary did not like her own looks because she looked too much like Aunt Sophia's daughter Catherine. Catherine had carrot red hair, freckles and light eyelashes and brows. Knowing how sensitive the younger girl was about this, she liked to comfort by pointing out the nice features of her young sister. It was Patricia, too, who would on occasion when there was news of a sick family member, relative or friend, Pat would gather the younger children. A candle would be lit, then picking up a prayer book, Patricia would lead all to pray for the sick.

A few weeks after the apple-tossing incident and the chat with her sister, Mary began to notice that Pauline, one of her classmates was a possible good friend. They either walked home together or took the street car. This new friend went to daily Mass, was kind and gentle and a very conscientious student. She was an excellent student in all subjects except math. That was Mary's favorite subject and they often discussed homework on their way home. Mary liked early mornings and decided she, too, would attend Mass before going to school.

One late fall cold and drizzly day, Pauline and Mary felt cold and as they arrived near Pauline's home, Mary's friend invited her to come into her home and warm up with a cup of hot cocoa. Of course, the invitation was gladly accepted. On entering the house, there was a large foyer free of furniture and uncovered floor. As they moved into the living room furnished with a few shabby chairs, Mary was led into into the kitchen, Mary was struck with the barrenness of the home. The kitchen however was warm and with the matching warmth of Pauline's young sisters and mother, Mary focused on the friendly greeting. The family was seated at a barren table with empty small vegetable cans. Only after she had been seated next to the mother did Mary realize her friend's family was using cans to hold cocoa. Mary, however, was given a cup containing hot cocoa. Although the beverage was not as sweet or rich as Mary was used to, the hot drink was a pleasant beverage on such a gold day. The three girls and mother chatted away as if they   were long time friends. Pauline's friendly family, delighted Mary. The conversation, friendliness and joy of the afternoon, convinced the Tantalo girl that she would now have a long time good friend.

"You are late today, did you have some problem at school?" enquired Josephine.

"No, mama, I was invited to stop at Pauline's. She invited me to have a cup of cocoa before I continued home. It was cold and I went in to warm up."

"How very nice. That was thoughtful of her. I'm sure you did thank her," answered the mother.

"Yes, Mama, I did. But Mama, She comes from a poor, poor family," confided the daughter.

Mary in her usual lengthy fashion described the furnishings of the home. The mother listened attentively to her daughter's graphic description of the home and her afternoon's experience.

After a pensive pause, Josephine responded, "Pauline's family is not poor, poor. There are many families that have even less than what they have. You must also think of another wealth that your new friends have. Families that are caring, kind and friendly are rich. I am happy that you have such a fine friend and do invite her to also come visit you."

Francis was a senior and sought the advice of his Guidance teachers. Lorenzo's son enquired as to the path he would follow, subjects he needed and colleges that would be appropriate. Since he was a fine math and science student, his advisor suggested engineering might be a fine field for him to consider. When he shared his dreams with Lorenzo, the father was overjoyed.

"Pepina, at last one of our children is following a worthwhile profession," confided Lorenzo. Josephine, too, was happy at the decision. She knew how disappointed the father was when his daughters were not interested in the teaching profession. Lorenzo's father was an engineer and Lorenzo had planned to follow in his father's footsteps by becoming an engineer. He was sure his children would also want to become teachers and engineers following ancestral careers.

Fridays of the last semester at Marshall High, honor students were dismissed early. On one of those Fridays, Francis and Mary were sitting in the living room and chatting when voices were heard coming from the kitchen. It was Prudence's day to spend with the Tantalo family. The loud greeting of Aunt Maria interrupted Josephine and Prudence's soft voices.

"You will rejoice with me. I have some good news. At last one of our children is considering marriage. My son Tony just left my house after he came to introduce me to his intended. Her name is Rene and they will be engaged in a few weeks.

She seems a lovely and fine girl but they have known each other only several weeks," Maria joyfully reported.

"That is very good news Maria," said Josephine.

"Is she Catholic?" questioned Prudence.

"She must be," replied Maria. "Irene and Tony are going to see the Pastor at St. Anthony's Church," added Aunt Maria.

"Our girls are older than Tony and yet they are not yet seriously considering marriage. That worries me. Doesn't that worry you, Josephine? Frances and Nancy should at least be thinking seriously about marriage. My Lucy is friendly with Mary Ferra. Her brother Salvatore likes Lucy. I'm sure that will be the next marriage." Continued Maria.   The conversation continued in more subdued tones and Mary could no longer hear what was being said. Frank lost interest right away. But the young girl could not wait to inform her older sisters. She immediately went into the store and told Pat that she had important news that could not wait.

Since the father was busy with customers and Pat was not occupied, both girls went into the empty office. Patricia was given an enhanced report of the conversation Mary heard.

"Aunt Mary is still talking to Mama and Grandma. Go into the kitchen and find out what is going on," advised Mary.

Patricia was very interested and found an excuse to approach the kitchen. As she came into the room, she was shocked at the remarks she overheard. It was Aunt Mary's voice.

"Josephine, both those men are interested in your girls. Encourage them to get interested. They can double date the way we did," advised Maria.

"I will never tell my girls. Lorenzo never never mentioned the men's request to meet with them. Nor did he ever suggest that they should be interested in getting married. This is not

Italy. Parents don't select their daughters' husbands," the upset Josephine replied.

"In a few years your son Frank will be out of college, find a job and then you will have two older unmarried girls at home," continued Maria.

Prudence had been listening without comment. She silenced both of them with her words of wisdom.

"Let's stop a minute and just pray that God will bless Tony and Irene. That is important now. Remember, Maria, these are bad times for the young. Jobs are scarce. Tony, although he completed college, has only a part time job driving a bakery truck. Better to pray and plan carefully. It is important to consider the children that will be born," responded Prudence. Silence followed. The grandmother made the sign of the cross and thus after a few brief prayers, the discussion ended. When Frances and Nancy were settled and reading in the upstairs rooms, Patricia recounted the conversation among the women. The younger girl, too, listened and made contributions. Frances seemed very indifferent and Nancy was smiling. Immediately, when the girls completed their tale, Nancy smilingly shared,

"Pa said something to us about the men asking for permission to come to the house and make known their intentions." Frances continued reading after a brief period of listening.

"Who are they and why didn't you tell us," asked Pat indignantly.

"Papa didn't take them seriously and neither did we. Pa just made a comment as they were passing by one evening while we were sitting in the back yard. He certainly didn't think they were suitable anyway and we thought it ridiculous." You know them. The guys that pass by the store and peer in," acknowledged the smiling Nancy.

"You mean Bushy Eyebrows and Mr. You Wanna Go Mad?" Enquired Patricia.

"You said it," added Nancy.

All the girls burst into laughter. Many times while the girls were working in the store and not busy with customers, the two would be boyfriends would peer through the store windows and stare at the girls. One day, while some of their cousins, Dominic, Victor and brothers were in the store, they in turn looked out and stared back at the men. That episode minimized the staring sessions. None of the young people knew who they were, therefore, adopted nicknames for the young men.

"Let's go down and tell mama," commanded Pat.

Laughingly, the three girls went downstairs and assured their mother that Aunt Mary didn't understand the situation at all. When the girls were ridiculing the two men, as was her custom, Josephine reminded them that it was wrong to laugh at people. It was a relief to the girls, however, to realize the mother was smiling and not over concerned.

9
Risky Peer Relationships, Communism

Information sources during the early twentieth century included reading materials and radio. Two local daily newspapers, and several magazines were regular subscriptions of the Tantalo family. Lorenzo and his wife enjoyed reading materials during the quiet evenings while the children were occupied with study or interests of their own. Her husband often interrupted Josephine's reading.

"Listen to this, Mussolini is starting a Fascist government in Italy. What a mistake that will be.

Restlessness was enveloping all of Europe. This was due in most part to the Great Depression and unemployment in Europe seemed to be even more widespread than it was in America.

Francis would soon be graduating and started searching avenues of employment in his field, that of engineering. Those last months before graduation were anxious times for the young man. Perceiving his son's disappointment in not having a job to look forward to, Lorenzo made a suggestion,

"Would you like to consider opening a paint store on the corner of Emerson and Avery Street," suggest the father.

"I would like that, at least until the economy picks up," agreed Frank.

In the meantime, Mary had been working part time in the accounting office of a department store. Several months before graduating from high school, she had discussed with her sisters the career path she wished to pursue.

"I plan to be a writer and am therefore going to take courses in journalism and writing," firmly stated Mary.

"That's even more impractical than an art career. How do you expect to find a job in the writer's market? There is even talk of Rochester having only one newspaper," advised her sister Frances.

"Why don't you accept the scholarship from the business school for now and maybe you can take courses as the job market picture changes," advised Patricia sympathetically.

Although Mary was disappointed in the suggestion given she did decide to follow the advice of the older girls. Her courses at the School of Commerce were not as rigorous as they would have been at a university. She was receiving some practical courses that allowed her on the job training while studying.

This middle child didn't have the ability to focus attention on work alone, like the older children did. She was constantly looking for opportunities elsewhere. Besides her studies and work, Mary never turned down an opportunity for fun time. There were times when she not only put herself at risk but also disturbed and worried her older sisters, especially Patricia. Later, when she was more settled and somewhat wiser, she recalled incidents that showed selfishness and thoughtlessness.

One of the clerks at the store where she was employed fascinated Mary. Vera, a sophisticated, street smart girl, was friendly, entertaining, and somewhat crude. As they were leaving the workplace one afternoon, Mary, on impulse, invited the girl to her home for dinner. The invitation was immediately accepted. It happened on an evening when all the children were there for dinner but Lorenzo was working late. Their cousin Victor was also a guest of the evening.

While dinner was being prepared, the boys, Nancy and Mary waited in the living room, listening to the radio. Vera, coyly asked the boys if she could sit next to them on the large couch, even though there were other vacant chairs and couches in the room as well as places next to Nancy and Mary. When dinner was ready, Nancy took charge.

"Vera, you will be sitting next to me at table, Frances will sit at your right. We can get better acquainted with you," said Nancy while leading the girl into the dining room.

Mary naively thought that Nancy admired the girl. Before Vera left for the evening, she invited Mary to her home for the following Sunday.

"How did you like Vera, isn't she charming?" asked Mary of her sister Nancy.

"Where did you get acquainted with her? Can't you sense how crude and unmannerly she is?" responded her sister Nancy.

"I agree with you," added Francis.

"She is kind of crazy," continued the cousin Victor.

"Well, she works in the store where my office is and she invited me to her house next Sunday. I can't say no after I already accepted the invitation," almost tearfully responded Mary.

"It's not a good idea to visit her, Mary," added Frank.

Pat, after the barrage of negative responses and feeling sorry for the young sister, offered,

"Don't worry, I'll go with you Mary. You tell her that I need to accompany you."

"Thanks Pat, I'm sure she must have nice parents," hopefully answered Mary.

The following Sunday, after dinner and with written directions to the home, Patricia and Mary set out to visit Vera. The house was on the other side of town. It was on a lovely tree lined street with beautiful homes. The young girl felt a sense of relief. When they approached the house, they mounted the front steps, rang the doorbell and waited for a little while before it was opened. Pat and Mary heard loud laughter and soon a smiling Vera appeared. She ushered them into the living room, passed the dining room and into a large kitchen. There were at least five men in the room along with Vera's mother and aunt. Patricia noticed a number of bottles of beer and glasses partially full on the table. There were no introductions.

"Dinner will be ready in a half hour, honey," a smiling over made up woman told Vera.

"OK, mama," responded the daughter.

"Let's go into the living room while my mother and aunt get dinner on the table," invited Vera.

The smiling girl took out her record collection and immediately began to play some of the popular songs. After listening to the music for what seemed about a half hour, Patricia was beginning to feel at ease and soon two men walked into the room, one offered the girls a drink. Pat said,

"We don't drink. We aren't eighteen yet and we made the confirmation promise." Answered Pat.

"Oh, you are Catholics," one of the men laughingly responded.

He put the glass down and began dancing with Vera.

Patricia nudged Mary, who also began to have a sense of unease.

"It is getting late and we do visit our grandmother Sunday's, Vera, sorry but we must be leaving. Thanks for showing us your record collection," Pat said as the two girls rose to leave.

"Oh, I'm sorry, I didn't know   dinner would be so late. Mary, I'll see you at work tomorrow," answered Vera.

The girls walked away silently for a short time.

"Mary, I think that is a bad house. There were too many men there. I don't blame Vera. It was a very strange group, didn't you think so?" questioned Patricia.

"I did feel funny when the men came into the living room. I think one of them was drunk. Pat, you told the man that I was not eighteen yet. I'm eighteen and you are twenty one," added the younger sister.

"I was kind of scared and didn't know what to do or say," laughingly answered Pat. Both girls spontaneously burst into laughter of relief.

"We said that we were going to visit grandma. That is a good idea and she will be happy to have family company. Aunt Rosie called mama this morning and said that gram was tired after going to Mass," the older girl suggested.

"She likes ice-cream. Let's stop and get her some," added Mary.

On the return, there were friends, cousins and neighbors gathered on the top floor. They were playing cards and listening to records. Mary lost no time introducing them to the afternoon's experience.

"It's a good thing I invited Pat to go along with me to Vera's house. We think she lives in a bad house," confided the young girl while glancing at the large audience with exaggerated alarm.

Patricia gave a vivid description of the afternoon's events. She, too, exaggerated a little and ended with,

"I think both Vera's mother and aunt are prostitutes."

"Maybe so, but you can't be sure so don't spread that dreadful fact," added Frances.

They had a topic for discussion for the rest of the evening with cousin Lucy often interjecting, "That is a terrible sin and you took a big chance," added Lucy time and time again.

Cousin Mae finally finished the discussion with, "she didn't know Vera's background. Anyway, it doesn't hurt to be kind to girls in that situation."

Another more alarming event that gave the older Tantalo girls a sleepless night occurred late summer. As was often the case, Mary and several friends paired off with boys to spend Sundays, horseback riding, row boating and visiting the booths at the nearby amusement park. They attended the Policemen's Mass, at six AM. After Mass the group would assemble outside St. Joseph's Church and board the bus to Irondequoit Bay. The Bay was a forbidden place for all the Tantalos as well as the Serafines since Jerry Cooney's drowning.

As soon as they all arrived at the amusement park, the young people paired off into couples. Mary without realizing how it happened was matched with an unknown young fellow. Early afternoons, couples would join forces and rent a rowboat. Mary, her partner Edward, Jane and Gerald made up one of the assembled pairs. Julie, one of Mary's friends, tried in vain to reassemble the pairs. She realized Mary's company was not the right choice for her friend.

Although the morning slipped by without any unpleasant situations, Mary had a sense of anxiety. Both boys seemed much too immature and irresponsible. The group always lagged behind the other group of friends. Conversation was not only boring but at times even unpalatable and crude. Jane was no help. She didn't encourage the boys to keep with the crowd but even encouraged the delay. By two o'clock in the afternoon, long passed the time their friends left for the trip across the bay, the last two couples finally got into the rowboat and began rowing across the turbulent waters.

"Perhaps it would be better for us to remain here rather than set out now. We usually return here by three o'clock," suggested Mary.

"We don't have to stay with the crowd," answered an agitated Jane.

In mid waters, Mary realized that she was correct in her assessment of the young men. Not only were they immature but also were unfamiliar with rowing. The rhythm was wrong, and they weren't on course at all. As darkness approached, the boys finally realized that they were in trouble. The guards kept commanding them to return to shore. There were no lights on the boat. It was a very frightening feeling for the young girl, especially when she realized she was not a swimmer.

The young people finally did get to shore with the help of two lifeguards leading them on a slow and shaky ride. Jane did very little to make the return trip less dreadful. She often let out high-pitched shrieks complaining of the cold and assured them they would all drown. Mary prayed.

When the group arrived at the amusement park, there was little activity. It was almost midnight and the last bus to town had left. Getting back to their homes was going to be a problem. Jane grew sullen, Mary began walking rapidly toward the bus route. Edward quickly began walking too.

"Are you going to walk home?" timidly enquired Edward.

"Do you have any other suggestions?" asked Mary as she walked briskly on.

Gerald and Jane soon followed. They had no choice. Afraid of being left alone, Mary tried hard to be pleasant. The trip back to their neighborhoods took most of the night. When Mary arrived home, exhausted, hungry and cold, she immediately mounted the stairs to her bedroom. Fortunately, doors were never locked. As she arrived at the top floor, her sisters met her. They were fully dressed with somber expressions. With gestures, they motioned her to one of the back bedrooms, anxious not to wake their parents or children on the floor below, they shut the door after entering.

"Where have you been? We have been up all night waiting for you," angrily questioned Frances.

"You went to the Bay again, didn't you?" I told you so many times how dangerous it was. I thought you had drowned," tearfully questioned Patricia.

"We were going to phone the police but didn't want to wake ma and pa," reprimanded Nancy.

Mary quickly told her story. Exhausted and weary, the morning came much too soon.

Reflecting on some of the past events, Mary became restless and decided some changes were needed. In a few weeks she would be completing courses at The School of Commerce. After a short time elapsed, she was hired to work for a large advertising firm.

"But the work is not in my field of study," responded Mary on knowing most of her work would be typing.

"You need to have experience other than sales," suggested the counselor.

It was a cold drizzly day in mid February the first day at the new job. She entered the factory like tall building and walked three flights of stairs to reach the advertising firm. A tall heavy-set woman approached her and immediately assigned her a small typing desk with large stacks of envelopes next to her place. At least ten other women were seated in like places. No formal welcome or introduction, the woman handed Mary a large stack of printed papers.

"These are customer addresses and the top box holds labels. You are to type labels and paste them on the envelopes," ordered the woman frigidly.

Since Mary had never intended to pursue a typing career but that of an accountant, she was a slow typist. Not only did she lack speed but the cold building made her stop periodically to rub her hands for warmth. The tall woman passed her desk very often that first day. Each time she examined the amount of work completed, she would exclaim,

"You will be owing us instead of we owing you on pay day."

When Mary arrived home at the end of the workday, she used the kitchen entrance. She did not want to meet her brothers and sisters. They would ask how her workday went. She hated the place and everyone working there. This new employee was ready to burst into tears.

Josephine was waiting for her daughter. She was the last to arrive and late for supper.

"Hang up your coat. wash your hands and sit down. Your meal is being kept warm. We had pork chops and steamed escarole, your favorites." With a warm smile and caring manner, the mother placed the warm dinner in front of the unsmiling daughter.

"Mama, I'm going to be fired. I hate the job and can't do the work," sobbed Mary.

Lorenzo walked into the kitchen and encouragingly said, "You don't need to work. There is always room for you to work for me." The father suddenly realized that his words did not comfort the girl.

"Best leave the mother to mend this hurt. I certainly don't know how to handle these problems," thought Lorenzo as he returned to his reading in the living room.

The mother, pouring coffee for both of them, sat next to her daughter taking her usual listening stance. Hot food and the mother's comforting presence gradually brought calmness to the daughter. Going to great detail, Mary explained the work situation to Josephine.

"It was brutally cold, all the workers were working frantically, trying to complete their work. They didn't ever look up from work and all I heard was the click, click of the typing keys. No linoleum or rug covered the floor, my desk was wobbly and the chair too high. Mama, the worst part was the boss lady. What a witch. She had a perpetual scowl, with a mean expression."

Her sister Frances interrupted Mary's tale.

"I suppose you got fired," interrupted Mary's sister Frances.

"No, she didn't get fired but it's not a good place for her to work. There was no heat in the building. She will not go back there. Find out if she can work in your office," the mother suggested.

"As a matter of fact, there are two openings at the office. Get up early tomorrow and come with me. We will be at work before eight. The boss gets there at seven o'clock and leaves by noon," offered the big sister.

The young girl was not sure she wanted to try another job so soon but she didn't want to be without work either. Some of her friends, having graduated from high school, were still unemployed. Frances was not an early riser and somehow had made arrangements to work from nine to five.

"I'll help her get started in the office with Jimmy. He is easy to get along with and isn't a slave driver. She can learn well under his tutelage. I think she needs to know that one can work and still be able to enjoy her day." Thought Frances. Anxious to be a success, Mary took Patricia side and confided in her concern about the interview the next day. Her sister assured her that she would like the place.

"You may not remember it, but I went to work there for two weeks. One of the girls in the office was ill and Jim needed a substitute for a little while. Jim is nice and so is Buzz. She is one of the office workers that I helped out," encouraged her sister.

It was a short bus ride to the workplace and Mary realized the building they were approaching was not unlike the factory building where she had her recent bad experience. When they entered the building, however, much to her surprise, they entered a warm, comfortable, well-lit large office. At the far end there were several other offices.

Leading her younger sister, Frances moved toward a handsome smiling young man seated behind a large desk.

"Wow, what makes you come in so early this morning?" teased the fellow.

"Jim, this is my sister Mary. She is going to fill in an application for the opening in this office. Can you give her an application? Explain the work needs and introduce her to the workers in the factory. Is the boss in?" questioned Frances.

"Sure, the boss is in. He's in a good mood, too, and thanks, Frances, for bringing your sister in," answered the young man.

The application didn't take long to complete and the young girl handed it to the office manager. He arose from his desk and after introducing her to a smiling Buzz, she was ushered into the factory. There were men and women operating large machines. Desks were scattered at different intervals. Frances' sister was introduced to at least forty employees. When they returned to the office, Frances was there teasing Buzz.

"What a nice atmosphere, I hope they hire me," thought Mary.

"Jim, Boby wants you in his office. We'll be here waiting for you," added Frances.

Picking up the application, Jim faced the three girls with crossed fingers and disappeared into the far office. Within a few minutes, Jim opened the door and motioned for Mary to come in. Mr. Crowford was a short older man, serious but with a pleasant expression.

"You will be working with Jim. Your sister said that you could begin immediately. There is a large backlog of work. Another worker will join you in several weeks," offered the boss. Ready to shout with joy, responding with very few words, Mary told the boss she was ready to start work immediately. Frances had already left but returned in a little while.

"You can have lunch with me today. I'll come when it's lunchtime. Join us, Buzz," ordered Frances.

After Frances' quick exit, the office staff's workday began. Within a few weeks, Mary felt very much a part of the work force and enjoyed her new job. Occasionally, employees would be dubbed with nicknames. Mary soon was referred to as Junior. The Boss couldn't always remember the names of new workers and on impulse would call them by an alias. Eventually he would begin calling them by their given names. Nicknames, however, stuck. One of the young men from the factory was called String Bean.

Weeks and even months just flew by. There were a number of employees in the factory that interested Mary. The group she ate lunch with included Buzz, String Bean, Adele, Larry, Glen and Susan. Susan was the new office worker that just had graduated from Mercy High. Frances lunched with elder workers at a later time.

Frequently a few of the group would meet after work Fridays and spend the evening dining at a restaurant. Usually, the choice of the eating place would be suggest by Glen. He often selected a place that included a music group. Dancing would be permitted if a cover charge were paid. Jazz was the in thing and all of them enjoyed dancing. The office staff worked Saturday mornings and Mary used that as an excuse to leave before 9:30 PM. Lorenzo made too big a fuss if the girls came in late. She didn't want to admit to her colleagues that her father was strict. Adele never accepted the invitation to join them.

There was a vacancy in the office and Mary shared this with her sister. "Frances, why don't you suggest that Adele be hired for the office vacancy? She is so intelligent, works hard and is very articulate. Her boyfriend is a doctor intern," suggested the younger sister.

"My gosh, don't you know that she is a Communist? She wouldn't accept the job anyway. She is working to start a union in the factory and wants to work, by her term, among THE MASSES," informed Frances.

"She is only a sympathizer, like the Costas," responded Mary.

"Not at all like the Costas. She is active," and with the brief statement, Frances dismissed the suggestion.

Mary had engaged Adele in many lively conversations as they rode the bus on the way home. She was awed at the knowledge this girl had. No subject was foreign to her. She was an attractive tall blond, dressed simply with a limited wardrobe and often spoke of the poor. Her parents were immigrants from Poland and Adele was the only child. A few months after Mary's suggestion to Frances, Adele invited the young girl for a Polish dinner at her home. Adele knew Mary was very fond of cabbage.

The home was comfortable and dinner was delicious. Mary and the girl's mother conversed during most of the meal while Adele was discussing factory information with the father. During the dinner the phone rang and after a brief interval, the father told his daughter the call was for her. It was a lengthy conversation. The mother and father were clearing the table and Mary offered to help. She remained alone in the kitchen helping with the dishes.

"I am so happy that you came for dinner. Please help my daughter. I'd rather she be dead than watch her get involved in the mess she is in," softly whispered the mother.

They had been discussing religion while working together in the kitchen. Mary assumed that either Adele had given up her religion or was having an illicit relationship with her fiancé. Adele's father offered to drive Mary home. While they were riding along, the daughter shared the content of her phone conversation.

"Dad, I'll be taking a train to New York City during the weekend. They are having a big meeting and I'll be representing the Rochester area."

"Will you be needing money? I'll be happy to help, you know," offered the father.

"No, funds will come from the Labor Lyceum functions," added the daughter.

As the father and daughter conversed animatedly all during the ride, Mary was confused and didn't understand the gist of the conversation. Fear that Frances was right, Mary questioned Patricia. She wouldn't reveal the source of information. Next evening, while they were helping prepare the evening meal, Mary question Patricia.

"Pat, what is the Labor Lyceum?"

"Communists hold their meetings there and often show movies to raise money for their activities. Usually they are propaganda movies. I went once with Mae to satisfy my curiosity," enlighten the sister.

"What a revelation that is," thought Mary.

Several days later, another invitation came from Adele.

"I know you like to dance. Why don't you come to a party in my neighborhood? You will like the young people. It will be next Saturday evening from six to nine. My father and I will pick you up at five thirty," invited the girl.

Mary consented without a moments thought. She regretted her impulsive acceptance but let it stand.

The dance was held at a small dance hall in the neighborhood. On arrival, Mary observed that the gathering of young people was not unlike other dances she had attended. Her father frowned on dances held at dance halls but they were not serving alcoholic drinks. Pitchers of lemonade and paper cups were on one of the side tables. That was the only source of refreshments being served. It seemed like an OK place to be, thought Mary.

As the evening wore on, Mary noticed that she was given an unusual amount of attention. Several young men invited the young girl to the dance floor. There was no lull of invitations and the young men seemed to be intelligent, well groomed and very attentive. Mary did look pretty that evening. She wore the light blue, many skirted dance formal. Libra, the hairdresser, had done a nice job on her auburn hair. Even her brothers said that she didn't look too made up. On leaving the house that evening, Josephine complemented her.

"You look very pretty. Have a nice time, don't get home too late."

The Tantalo girls always took pride in their appearance. Sisters as well as mother were always there to advise, encourage and complement them. Friends, too, often took time to discuss clothing, colors, hairdressers and good clothing shops.

It was not the first time that Mary had attended a dance but the unusual attention did puzzle her. Several of the young men suggested future dates, asking for her phone number and assuring her that they would keep in touch. Within a few months, Mary attended two dances. Adele and two other fellows with impeccable manners always picked her up.

Another invitation that was accepted, however, completely surprised, alarmed and disappointed Mary. There would be a gathering at Adele's home.

"You know most of the young people. I'm sure you will have a lovely time. You are accepted in our group and have many good friends there," advised Adele. It will be just a small gathering. There isn't too much room at my house.

Bill, Jenny and Todd will pick you up at 5:30," Adele told Mary.

Many of the guests had arrived already and Mary sat on the couch next to a smiling Bill. The group was listening to a recorded Mozart's selection. This was an unusually large living room with at least three big couches, several winged chairs and a huge table at one end of the room. Jenny and Todd were placing stacks of flyers on the table. Finally, all were seated, the music selection ended and conversation began.

A tall handsome light haired youth rose and interrupted the chatter. "I have written a poem that may interest you."

It was a scholarly, lengthy sonnet, including many figures of speech, metaphors and alliterations. It was a beautiful poem. It was read brilliantly with just the right inflections. The substance was about an abandoned cold barn that housed Mexican farm hands. They didn't have bus fare to return to their homeland. It was a touching, sad poem. It was so moving, that Mary and many of the girls were sobbing. Mary never learned the name of the young poet or did she ever hear or see the poem in writing.

After a short time Adele spoke,

"That was beautiful. Many like poems could be written about the damages of capitalism. We will have a brief pause for refreshments and then we can start our meeting. Thanks, Jane for planning our entertainment for the evening." With the quick and short remark, Adele left the room. Silently, chairs were being moved into a circle, paper cups, napkins and small paper plates were distributed. A strange flag was hoisted up.

Adele's mother made her first appearance. Unsmilingly, holding a large platter of cookies, the mother served the young people and the daughter followed, filling glasses with lemonade. When the mother and Adele served Mary, they quickly moved on without uttering a word. Mary feebly said, "thank you." For a few minutes she was experiencing a panicky feeling. When the mother and daughter left the room, Mary boldly rose from her place and followed them into the kitchen. Directing the words to Adele's mother Mary spoke up,

"May I help?"

"So you, too, are one of them," responded the mother, coldly turning away from the young girl.

Returning to the room, Adele with a firm and no nonsense tone of voice began delegating tasks to individuals.

"Todd, how many churches are you going to cover tomorrow?" she questioned.

"I'm covering the Lake Avenue section. The Lutheran church, Christian Science on Seneca Parkway and Sacred Heart at Flower City Park," answer Todd.

Like assignments continued until all were given flyers. Adele then smilingly turned to Mary, "Why don't you give out flyers at your church, tomorrow? One church is enough for the first time.

Mary felt like a defensive school child and feebly answered, "My father will not let me do that."

"That's fine, it's your first time. Better wait until the next meeting. Each of you will receive a packet. There is reading material that is very informative. Try to read it all. It is information that will help us educate the masses," added Adele.

Chairs and other furniture were put into place and with not too much chatter, young people, with a quick, "good-by" left the home. Mary, not comfortable, said to Adele,

"That was a Communist meeting. May I use the phone? I'll order a cab. I can get home without an escort.

Of course you may use the phone. But please let me go along with you and Bill," Adele answered with a deeply concerned tone. Mary, realizing she would continue seeing the girl at work each day, consented. Adele led the conversation on the way home. The meeting, was not mentioned. Topics included music and some of the their favorite composers.

Using the Kitchen entrance, Mary found Nancy and Pat sitting on the corner table having a warm drink. Joseph and Freddy were at the large table writing.

"Hurry and finish up Popin and Freddy. You waste so much time evenings and wait until it's bed time to finish your homework," scolded Nancy.

Glancing her way as she opened the door, Nancy spoke up,

"What's the matter? You are as white as a ghost. Are you sick?"

"No, I had a bad experience," answered the younger sister.

"Let's go in the dining room. We won't wake up the others. You two, get finished and get to bed. Don't let mama call you a hundred times before you get up to go to school," ordered Nancy.

As soon as they were seated, Mary handed the packet of literature to her sister Nancy. She gave them background information on the previous encounters with Adele, the warning from Frances that Adele was an active Communist and then proceeded to tell her evening's experience.

"Please don't tell Frances. I don't want Adele to get fired. She has such a fine mother. I feel so sorry for that poor woman. Maybe I can help Adele.

"You can't help Adele. She's been well trained and once they are obsessed with the cause, that's it," exclaimed Nancy.

The girls spent some time examining the literature and as they were interrupted by sounds in the kitchen, they rose, gathered the papers and Nancy held out her hand for those held by Pat and Mary. After the boys left the kitchen, Nancy went toward the cooking stove.

"The embers are still hot. Let's dump the papers into the fire. Best get rid of them right away. Pa will have a fit if he sees them. He calls Communists revolutionaries and anarchists. He thinks they try to overthrow our government. Maybe he is right. At least I think some of them do get carried away with fool philosophies".

Mary was grateful she didn't have to face Adele the next day. Sunday would give her time to calm down before she faced Adele at work.

10
Jim Crow Laws, Rumors of War, the Draft

"Turbulent times seem eminent," thought Lorenzo. He had been reading the papers, listening to Radio news and broadcasts. There was every indication that young men would be drafted. Rationing of certain food items had already started. Fear that another war was on the horizon, Lorenzo knew that some of his boys would be in the midst of combat. His children, however, seemed to be unaware of the seriousness of the situation.

Francis, though, seemed to have a sense of urgency. Talk of war and the draft among his classmates assured them that their country would soon be joining nations already at war. Soon after graduation, he opened a branch of his father's store. Within a few months he was courting a young girl. Irene's family lived in Malone, a small town, in the North Country, near the Canadian border. She came from a large family and was a daughter of French immigrants. Francis lost little time introducing her to his family. Like many of their friends, they planned a quick and simple wedding. Lorenzo was disappointed feeling his son was not well enough established to take on the responsibility of a family. Josephine, however, was delighted.

"She is a lovely girl, Catholic and goes to Mass daily.

Let's go to Malone and visit the family," Josephine suggested.

Frank drove his parents as well as his girl friend to Malone. They spent a week in the area. Lorenzo was fascinated with the expanse of underdeveloped land, the beauty of the mountains, reminiscent of the little village he came from. Josephine, too, liked the small villages. Conversations with the girl's parents were manageable even though Irene's parents spoke French and little English. There was some similarity between the Italian and French languages. Both fathers, however, spoke English most of the time. Satisfied, the parents returned to Rochester, happy that their son had selected a good partner. Soon after their marriage, the couple drove to the North Country frequently. Irene missed her family, relatives and friends. Francis thought of the girl's loneliness if he were drafted. He discussed the possibility of moving the store to the North Country. Lorenzo, of course, was pleased. He had considered it while they had been visiting there. He knew Frank liked to drive and was sure the couple would visit Rochester often. The North Country became a frequently visited vacation place.

Dom and Mary who habitually looked to the older brother for support missed Frank. They however, as was customary with the young, went along with the changes in their lives. Dominic was searching for his own path and for a little while was considering getting into the same business ventures his father had already established. He was also considering attending college in California where Aunt Tonia's family lived. Soon after Frank was drafted, Dominic decided he would enlist in the Army rather than interrupt his studies. "I'll serve my time and then study," thought Dom.

Several other changes were also taking place in the household. Nancy and Frank Long were thinking of getting married. Frank worked as an accountant in the neighboring fuel company. Frances was planning a career change. Although she liked her work, she felt there was no future where all credits and accompanying raises were given only to the engineers. She started training to become a real estate agent. Interest in real estate became a major preoccupation for the first-born Tantalo child.

"Mama, I am thinking of buying a small house of my own. I'm not interested in any fellow right now and I'd like my own place. One of the women at work is getting married and is selling her cottage for a very reasonable price," said Frances.

The mother responded wistfully, "My children are growing so fast. I still think of you as my little ones. You will be missed by me, the other children and especially grandma. She is always asking for you."

"I'll be only a few streets away and you won't even notice that I'm not living here. You know I'll be here often.

Besides, I think I'll be here for all my meals. I can't and don't like to cook." The mother smiled, realizing that Frances, indeed, did not like to cook.

In view of the fact that her sister was soon going to work elsewhere, Mary decided to search for employment in accounting.

"Jim, *I have been working* here two years. As much as I'd like to stay here, I need to get into the field where I was educated. I'm just beginning my search and I thought it only fair that you become aware of my interest."

War news was not only disturbing but it seemed President Roosevelt was leaning toward plunging the country into another war. Many young men were being drafted. Others enlisted. Ammunition factories and other industries related to the war effort were initiated. There were vacancies in many industries due to the drafting of young men. Jobs that were usually held by men were now being taken over by women. Many accounting jobs were available and Mary was carefully considering the pros and cons of each position. Working for a large company that was national in scope seemed to appeal.

After discussing the options with her sisters, she decided to work for Armour, a national meat and dairy products company.

"How do you like your new job?" questioned Nancy.

"I'm fascinated with figures, profit and loss can be very revealing. It's great getting into the field that I really feel competent. Every Monday morning I meet with the factory manager, office manager and the big boss. I report on the profit or loss of each item. I then need to give my opinion on reasons why each product was less or more profitable than the previous week. Of course, as an ingredient's price rises, a comparable loss will be evident. The same goes for the drop in price of a component. I find that very enlightening," animatedly answered the younger sister.

Weeks and months sped by quickly. Mary enjoyed her employment and joyfully went to work each day. On one particular morning she found herself in an embarrassing situation. It was one of those beautiful sunny spring May mornings. Wearing a new outfit, a red and white checked dress with matching accessories, she actually began skipping as she was walking toward the bus stop, thinking she was the only pedestrian on the street. She was surprised by a husky male voice behind her.

"Be careful, young woman, you will surely trip if you continue skipping with those high heeled shoes," a male voice was heard behind her.

"Yes, you are right, Mr. Miller," she timidly replied. The young girl recognized the owner of the large furniture factory. Neighbors living in the area before the turn of the century told fascinating stories of the man. Jacob Miller had little formal education and his father was the ragman. In olden times, a horse drawn wagon driver would buy worn clothing for a few pennies a pound. The wagon would appear several times a week. Frequently, Jacob, the handsome young boy, would ride along and help his father. Jacob Miller, the now wealthy factory owner, was held in high esteem. He visited his old neighborhood, greeted old folks and sometimes even stopped to chat.

As she continued on her way to the bus stop, Mary thought, "that sure was stupid of me. Good thing he doesn't know me. But it is such a beautiful day and how nice to have a job that I like." The young woman always attended Mass before continuing on her way to work. St. Joseph's Church was near Armour's. That morning she thanked God for the beautiful day, having a job she liked and kind employers like Mr. Miller. Jacob Miller's workers, most of them immigrants, found him generous, kind and a man that often praised his employees

Scanning the newspaper one evening, Mary read an article that interested her. The university was offering evening classes in radio and television. The young girl, thinking this was an invitation to script writing courses, decided to apply for the class. Meeting her friend, Helen, at the bus stop the next morning, Mary confided,

"Helen, I am going to sign up for writing courses after work this evening."

After a brief explanation of the news item, Helen responded,

"Do you mind if I go along, I might be interested too?" added her friend. Mary was delighted to have her friend accompany her. The girls were surprised that classes had been in session for a few days. The registrar suggested they attend the evening's class due to begin in half an hour.

They entered the empty classroom early and before long the instructor met them. He questioned them on their employment as well as educational background.

"We have had several sessions and you may be floundering at the start, but I'm sure you can get caught up. If need be, I can help after class. I remain in the building for about a half hour after this period."

When students began taking places in the large room. It was evident before the start of class that only men were taking the course. Helen, with her large dark expressive eyes looked over to Mary with an awed look.

Mr. Ward, the instructor, was sketching a diagram on the black board as students were walking in.

"What is he drawing on the board? It reminds me of the physics class I had in high school. I hated physics and received my worst marks in that subject," thought Mary. The lecture began with explaining functions of copper wiring, tubes, etc. Near the end of the session some Morse code messages were listed on the board. Observing the students around her taking notes and copying sketches, Mary followed their examples. As soon as the end of the period bell rang Mary hurried out of the room with Helen rapidly following her. They were silent until they were out of the building.

"What was that all about?" enquired Helen.

"I suppose understanding function of equipment parts is necessary in script writing. Timing is an important element if a play needs to fit into a station's programming schedule," suggested Mary.

Both girls soon found out that the course was truly a class in radio and television equipment maintenance. After class, Helen went to Mary's home where the girls worked on assignments and discussed the possibility of dropping out of the course. At the start of the second week of class both girls resolved to report to the office after class and drop out of the course. When they walked into the classroom, what was to be their last day, cameras were set up and two men were talking to Mr. Ward.

"Here are the two women in my class." With that Mr. Ward introduced the bewildered young women to reporters.

Both girls were questioned.

"Why are you women taking courses usually taken by men?" questioned one reporter.

"I intend to work for American Airlines. I hope to get a job working at the control towers," unflinching answered Mary's friend.

Mary was astonished at the cleverness of Helen's answers. One of the responses had consequences that introduced many unexpected events in her young friend's life.

Within a few days an article that included pictures appeared in the local paper. It placed the girls in a position that made it awkward to terminate the course in equipment maintenance. More surprisingly, one evening the airlines contacted Helen. She was to appear at one of their offices for an interview. Helen was ultimately a shy person and needed affirmation. Mary's friend lived with her widowed mother, five sisters and a brother. She suggested Mary take a day off from work and accompany her when she went for the interview.

"Helen, you would make a very poor impression if you needed someone to be with you. Do you really want to work for an airline?" questioned her friend.

"My boss isn't that fond of me and is always threatening to fire me. I'd like to work for the airlines. My cousin works in a control tower. He is very interested in the course I'm taking."

At the end of the semester, Helen went to Buffalo, trained as an operator and managed to remain on the job for many years.

The war years diminished the number of men available and companies were hiring women to replace the draftees.

With rumors of war, young men enlisted and girls were quick to replace men folks at jobs. Travel became popular and Mary noticed a decided change of personnel at Armour's. She was given several promotions with accompanying raises. She reflected on the number of young men leaving, "Wow, it's great that I am getting promotions," passed through her mind. Immediately she reminded herself that there might soon be a war, men would be killed and was saddened at the future of these fine young men. Her brothers, too, were considering enlisting. Promotions and raises soon lost their appeal.

Changes were also taking place in the accounting department. Rationing of food brought about an additional task of balancing rationing points as well as cash. Different methods were being experimented with. The office manager suggested Mary travel to other company offices along the Eastern section of the United States. She was assured the travel expenses would be borne by the company. Lorenzo refused to give his consent on his daughter traveling alone.

"If one of your sisters will go with you, fine, but no child of mine is traveling to unfamiliar places," was the father's response.

Traveling with the younger sister did not appeal to her sisters, besides, they   could not take time off from their jobs.

"Why don't you take Stella? She is from Texas. You will be going there as one of your stops. Her parents would be comforted by her visit," suggested Josephine.

Stella was a friend of Mary's, who had moved to Rochester looking for work. The office Manager assured Mary that travel expenses would include enough for a traveling companion. Both girls were excited and enthusiastic over the plans and immediately set out to get ready for the two-week trip. Trains were to be the mode of travel with the exception of a few small towns that had bus routes only. While Mary visited offices, Stella shopped, visited the town or remained at the hotel. The first few days were not only profitable for Mary but also enjoyable. A sudden change took place. Mary's friend became sullen and defensive. It started at the train station at St. Louis.

Two women, a black girl and a white one were having a heated argument. Both women were arguing over their rights. Mary became aware of the problem. Two side by side rest rooms, each clearly marked in bold letters, WHITE WOMEN, the other BLACK WOMEN. It was quite apparent that the unbelievable was really true. In some sections of the United States, Jim Crow Laws were enforced.

"My goodness, they have Jim Crow laws. Isn't that awful!" the alarmed girl said looking at her friend from Texas.

"That black girl had no business using the women's lav. That is what is awful," the agitated Stella responded.

The happy climate of camaraderie was quickly dissolved. Mary became nervous. Many more such incidents would occur during the trip. There was definitely a climate of hostility.

When the two girls were near the end of the business trip, with Forth Worth being the last stop, both girls were preparing to visit Stella's parent's home. A bus was boarded to reach the small town outside of the big city. The bus trip revealed large fields of flat land with an occasional house. There were also large cattle ranches along the way.

Stella gave the signal for the bus to stop. They were in front of a small house. A smiling elderly man and woman reached for the luggage. Stella, turning to her mother, gently admonished, "Mama, we can carry our own luggage." The parents tearfully hugged their daughter.

"Stella, how happy we are to see you. Thank you, Mary for helping my daughter find a job and I'll always be grateful that your mother suggested you bring our daughter along."

The house was modest, spotlessly clean and an aroma of good cooking permeated throughout the small-unpainted cottage. After the girls deposited the luggage in their assigned rooms, they were invited to sit down for dinner. It was a delicious meal. After the dinner cleanup, Mary suggested that Stella remain to give detailed information on her friends and job in Rochester. The mother was assured Mary needed time to get caught up on her notes. After working at a table alone for a few hours, Stella's father finally joined her. Again, his daughter's friend was thanked profusely.

It was apparent that the folks were not only lonely but were also having deep financial problems.

"My children all left home as soon as they reached a workable age," confided the father. He continued in a soft tone,

" We have four children, three boys and Stella. All the boys left home as soon as they finished their studies. Big cities with big money jobs appealed to them. This is a ten-acre farm. My wife and I spent all our savings to purchase this land. We were sure the boys would divide the land and have a little to start with when they married. This is a peanut farm. The crop began to go bad around the start of the depression. We didn't have money to improve the crop. See that jar by the fireplace? Those were picked from our land."

He rose from his chair and had Mary examine them. They were half the size of the peanuts the girl was familiar with. He continued,

"Peanuts were much larger when we first farmed. Now the soil is bad and no way can we get back the quality of former shipments. It would take more money than we can ever pay back." Mary had no words to comfort the old man. This kind of farming was so unfamiliar to the young woman.

Stella seamed so relaxed and happy that Mary thought,

"They seem so happy to see their daughter. I'll try to forget any of the incidents that occurred on the trip. Stella needed this trip and so did her parents," Mary promised herself. It was much more difficult to keep her promise than she would have ever imagined. In fact, on the return trip to the big city, a surprise awaited Mary.

While sitting on the bus the two girls were conversing amicably and the bus suddenly stopped in front of a large make shift empty shack. At least twenty people, men women and many children boarded the bus. It was a hot August day, all were barefoot, had smudged hands, faces and carried brown burlap sacks. The adults had colored handkerchiefs and were wiping their sweaty faces.

Startled, Mary turning to Stella said, "What poor, poor people. They must be migrant workers. I heard about them but never realized how bad off they really are. How sad."

"They are only Peons, don't get near them. They have lice," disgustedly answered Stella.

"How can Stella be so kind and loving at home and still be so mean minded when it comes to people that differ from her. Better that I keep my mouth shut. I just don't understand." Thought Mary. The rest of the bus trip was spent with Mary writing notes and Stella dozing.

Only two more office stops were scheduled one in Dallas and the last in Austin, Texas. Saturday would be the last day of gathering information. The girls arrived in Austin mid morning Friday. The hotel stay was delightful. It was such a beautiful town, the hotel personnel were gracious and hospitable. Eating at the hotel restaurant was a delight. Several black couples were seated in the same room with the girls and white waiters were serving them just as genially as they did on white customers.

Dallas, however, was a disaster. The morning went well enough, the Armour accountants over extended themselves and made sure the young woman from the North had all the needed information. Mary was tired when she arrived at the hotel that last day of work. Stella was not at the hotel. Mary spent time finishing notes and was ready to rest and listen to the radio. Since they would be leaving after Mass on Sunday, she packed, and selected clothing to be worn on the return trip home. She was surprised to notice she did not have a hat for church. When Stella returned and they were getting ready to go out for a meal, Mary suggested,

"Stella, I don't have a hat to wear for church tomorrow.

I'd like to shop for one after our meal," suggested Mary. Smiling approvingly, Stella offered, "Let's go to N. Markus. It's a great store. I never shopped there but I have heard it is one of the best," offered Stella. They agreed on a restaurant close to the shopping area. Again, very conspicuously noticed blacks were seated apart from the whites. A drinking fountain was close to the entrance of the store, again a large printed sign was posted just above the fountain, WHITES ONLY. A young black boy was sobbing while the mother pushed him away from the water fountain.

"Our drinking water is on the other side. We'll get there soon," comforted the mother.

Shopping after their meal became a tedious chore. First of all, Mary's personal money was fast dwindling. The hat display was unbelievable. Nancy made her hats and only charged for the materials. Ten dollars during pre war times for a hat was quite a price to pay for the least expensive one on display. It was a cheap straw with no style.

Leaving for Rochester after Sunday Mass, the girls silently boarded their last train trip to Rochester.

The train was not air-conditioned, the dining car was crowded and noisy. Though hungry, Mary had no appetite. Stella seemed not to mind and for that Mary was grateful.

Arriving at the Rochester train terminal, Mary turned to Stella and ended the trip, "thanks for accompanying me on the trip. I did get more information than I expected," said Mary.

"You must know that I should be very grateful to you. My parents really were so happy to see me. My mother feels better now that she knows I have a good friend if I need one," sincerely added the young friend from the South.

Josephine, Mary's mother was relieved to have her daughter home.

"You look so tired. Did all go well for you?" The worried mother asked.

"Mama, Stella's Mother said to be sure to thank you. It was good that she visited her family. Her parents felt relieved when they saw her and she told them how much she likes her work." Mary decided she would not mention the distasteful events that took place on the trip.

11
World War Two, Soldiers, Sailors, WAACS, WAVES

Neighborhood transformations were gradually taking place pre war years. Fewer young children played out doors, horse drawn carriages were seen and middle and low-income families were purchasing many more cars. Cobble stone roads were being replaced with brick or tar paved streets. Electricity-lit homes were replacing gaslight and more neighbors had phones. Phone conversations came over several lines. A party line lacked privacy since neighbors could pick up the phone and listen in.

The four youngest Tantalo children were fast reaching young adulthood. Joseph had just enlisted in the Navy. Cousins, too, were searching for future career roads. The younger cousins were Josephine's brothers' children. Uncle Lazarus' oldest boy, George, was already going to the minor seminary and was very secure in his decision to become a priest. Uncle John's oldest boy, Dominic, however, had tried the Franciscan seminary and quickly decided the priesthood was not for him. Pierrina, the first-born daughter of Uncle John, was always referred to as the nun in the family. Perry, as she was called, was not only pretty, an excellent student, a talented piano player but also had a beautiful, gentle and lovable disposition. During Perry's college graduation party, Mary asked her cousin,

"Perry, When are you going to the convent?"

"I have no intention of becoming a nun," immediately answered the young cousin.

"Grandma was sure you would be a nun. You know she always referred to you as the <u>MONICA</u>," countered the older cousin, Mary.

"I'm getting married some day. I want lots of children too," added Perry.

"Grandma died just two years ago and she always prayed that there would be a nun and priest in the family," Mary informed the younger girl.

"Well, you enter the convent then. I've just applied for a teaching job, and I was assured that I would certainly be employed at MCC," firmly answered the young cousin.

This came as a super shock to others in the party. After a brief pause, the party   continued with laughter, music and fun. Mary, however, was quite disturbed. She turned to her cousin George.

"Aren't you surprised at Perry's statement?" asked the older girl.

"Well, she can't help it if everyone thought she would become a nun. I never heard her mention that she would. Why don't you become one. It might not be a bad idea," added the seminarian.

Unbelievable at the statement, Mary soon left the party and shared her thoughts with her friend Helen. After a lengthy account of the party and her disappointments she confided,

"Helen, God has really blessed our family. I'm sure Grandma's prayers were very powerful. I am upset that Perry is giving so little thought to religious life.

The close friend, after a long discussion on the pros and cons, still left Mary very unsettled. She silently decided that she would pray over it. Maybe her cousin would eventually change her mind. Pauline, another close friend of Mary's who often spoke of becoming a Trinitarian Sister, was Mary's next confidant. The quiet Pauline didn't seem to help either although she suggested that Mary speak to a priest.

Work, leisure time activities and day-to-day routine dimmed her disappointment for a while. Mary continued enthusiastically, contented to carry on from day to day.

Just a few weeks remained before Helen would be living in Buffalo as an employee of the airlines. An invitation came from Mary's friend Helen,

"I need you to come with me Saturday evening. Do you remember Henry and Alfred, the two students of our Radio classes? We went out to dinner with them several times. They invited us to dinner next Saturday. Henry is going to phone you. Please come along. I don't want to go alone with Alfred."

"OK, but I really don't enjoy Henry's company. He is so pompous and always teases me about going to daily Mass. I'll go though. At least you and Alfred will be with us. Alfred has a knack of changing the conversation to some interesting topics," Mary responded. Both girls enjoyed the evening. The dinner was delicious and the music was super at <u>The Old Spain</u>, Helen's favorite restaurant.

Soon after the dinner date, in fact the following Sunday, Henry rang the door bell at Mary's home. A smiling Josephine met him at the door and admitted him into the living room where Uncle Lazarus was playing the piano.

"I just thought I would drop in for a short visit," Henry said to Mary's mother. Mary certainly was taken by surprise. The young fellow made himself at home. In fact he was dropping by for pop visits often. On one particular afternoon, family members were discussing the Thanksgiving holiday celebration. The conversation took a strange turn. Suddenly Henry confided,

"I'll be staying home I suppose, I'm not traveling to my home in Cleveland for just a day. I'm working Friday,"Henry added.

"There will be good food here. You can join us,"suggested one of the younger cousins. Mary knew that he would accept the invitation and was annoyed that Henry took so much for granted. He phoned several times before the holiday arrived but Mary declined his invitations to go out to dinner with him. He did show up on Thanksgiving day. After greeting the members of the family that were in the living room, waiting for dinner, Henry asked for Mary. Lorenzo was in the room conversing with Uncle Lazarus. When Mary walked into the room, Henry presented Mary with a tiny gift wrapped package.

"Open it," invited Henry.

An embarrased young woman opened the small box while her Father, Uncle and several cousins were looking on. Shocked at what was in the box, Mary was truly speechless.

"I'ts an engagement ring," a smiling Henry informed the watching group of relatives. Patricia, walking in while Mary was opening the package, knew that this was a surprise that was sprung on her younger sister. To ease the tension her sister was in, Patricia suggested,

"Let's go and show it to others that are in the kitchen." Leading her sister, she whispered,

"I bet he never even told you about it did he?"

"No, and I'd have given it right back to him. But you know what our aunts and uncles would say,"

"If you go out with a young man you must be considering marriage. They are so old fashioned about such things."

"Just wait a while, I'm sure there is a way out of this mess," encouraged Pat.

When most of the company left after the festivities, and a few guests were still in the kitchen helping with the cleanup, Mary went to the door with Henry.

"I'll pick you up tomorrow after work and we can go out to celebrate," suggested Henry.

"Let's make it Saturday evening instead," offered Mary.

"That will buy me time," she thought. Some miserable days followed. Josephine enquired, sensing something was not just right. "Do you like Henry?" questioned the mother.

"Mama, he is not Catholic and I really didn't go out with him that often," confided the daughter.

"This country will soon be at war. It's not good to be engaged with such uncertainty," wisely advised the sympathetic mother. It planted a thought in Mary's mind.

"I wish Dom or Frank were around. They would know how I could get out of this," mused Mary. Francis had been drafted, had been in the Army for almost two years and Dom enlisted soon after.

Patricia consented to go on double dates every time Henry invited her young sister out for dinner and the theatre. To include another couple every time they dated, Mary informed Henry that her father was strict. She suggested her sister go along or another couple be included on the date. It was on just such a double date, shocking news jolted the diners. After the main course, Henry's friend John, was suggesting desserts to complete the dinner, an announcement came over the loud speaker.

"Attention all, please listen to the radio broadcast."

President Roosevelt's voice came over the waves. The country was at war. There was an attack at Pearl Harbor.

"We need to go home right now. Our brothers are certainly going to be in the fighting. Pa and Ma will be very worried. Let's go home." suggested Pat.

"Pat's right," agreed John. "Take the girls to the car Henry, I'll pay the bill and be right with you," offered the friend.

When the girls arrived home all members of the family were hovered over the radio, listening to the news. Josephine quickly departed in search of the last letters from the boys. All

118

letters were vague about their whereabouts but Dom for certain was in the Pacific area. There was deep concern. In his last letter, Dom could not reveal his whereabouts. Josephine and Lorenzo soon received a phone call from Francis. He was still in the States. He enquired about his younger brother. He, too, was quite concerned.

Mary recalled the last time she had spoken to her brother Dominic. It was a warm summer Sunday afternoon and she was on her way to visit her friend Pauline. Dom was driving by and offered to drive her. While they were discussing family, friends and work, Mary's younger brother confided,

"I'm going to enlist in the army some time soon. Say a prayer Pa will approve. I'd rather get the military over before continuing studies. I'd like to study at one of the California Universities. That's where our cousins, the Martinos live."

"I'm sure Pa will approve. He is very patriotic. I have been considering going to the Convent. I'm not too sure about it right now. I plan to wait for a while anyway. I might even change my mind. I am still waiting for Perry to make up her mind. I can't believe she doesn't want to be a nun,"

Mary remembered confessing to Dominic.

As the family listened to news of the unexpected war with Japan, other members recalled memories of Dom. All were troubled that the quiet, industrious and gentle boy would be in the midst of a fight he was not trained for. Quiet predominated most of the households. "Pray for the boys," was an often-used phrase. Church attendance increased dramatically.

Concrete evidence that it was wartime began to emerge. Longer lists of foods required ration stamps. Victory gardens were being planted. Cotton stockings replaced the silk and nylons. Evening black-outs, sirens and wardens checking for infractions often alarmed young children. Very few young men were seen in the neighborhoods. These adjustments were constant reminders of the fighting and of the impending danger of loved ones.

Anxiety and uncertainty of Dom's whereabouts began to take its toll on Josephine. With the rosary almost always twined around her fingers, or sitting quietly reading from a prayer book was the constant stance of the sorrowing mother.

Her daughters often joined her and with a quiet exchange of smiles, silently gathered in the living rooms. Many planned celebrations were put on hold or canceled.

Letter writing was a continuous pastime. Mothers frequently shared news when a letter arrived from a soldier or sailor. Some sense of relief came to the Tantalos after letters arrived from Francis, Joseph and Fred. Nothing was heard for their son Dominic. Mail and packages were returned with notice: <u>Missing In Action.</u>

Lorenzo's days were spent writing Washington, the Red Cross and all agencies that dealt with the military. The father of the four Tantalo boys serving their country, closed the store early. He would read all papers and magazines with articles related to the war.

"How useless and costly these wars. Self-serving leaders driven by lust for power or greed bring about all wars," he would often remark. Many   times he would go into the kitchen or living room and read aloud to his wife. Daughters remained home more evenings. The younger Tantalo girls, Lucy and Amy began to take on many of the household chores. They, too, were more pensive and studious. Reading became the favorite pastime.

Occasionally soldiers and sailors would be on short furloughs. This was precious time spent with family members. Many neighbors and relatives were in the service.

When a military man came home, these young men visited relatives, and friends in addition to their own parents and family.

After warm greetings, they tried to comfort and reassure parents and families of their loved ones in combat.

Social events were minimized but activities were carried on to join in the war effort. Young women were considering war careers. Soon after the start of war, Mary received a letter from her friend Helen. She was being sent to North Africa to serve as a WAAC. Other friends of Mary went to Washington, serving as WAACS (women's army auxiliary corps) and WAVES (women accepted for volunteer emergency service). Most of them did clerical work usually done by men in the military. Army and Navy men were released from desk jobs. These men were assigned active combat duty. Several of these women, neighbors, cousins and friends of the Tantalo children remained in the service until retirement. WAACS and WAVES also had furloughs and visited family and friends. They, too, wore military uniforms. Their cousin Mae Serafine enlisted as a WAVE and remained in the service until retirement.

Social life had changed significantly for Mary. Like many of her friends, dancing, dinner dates and plays lost much of their appeal. Women were spending more time with neighbors, friends and relatives. They exchanged letters, shared their concerns and problems. When Mary wasn't working, writing letters or spending leisure time reading, she visited friends and relatives. When stopping in to visit Uncle Lazarus and Aunt Angie one Saturday afternoon, she asked the young seminarian, George,

"I'm considering returning Henry's engagement ring. An unmarried young military man should be free to date girls living near training camps and spend time writing their families. Better they are unencumbered with additional responsibilities," suggested the cousin Mary.

"Well, if you are asking for advice, I would say that is as good an excuse as any to get out of the engagement," responded Mary's young cousin. The young girl was troubled by the response and decided she would visit her friend Julia. Maybe she could help her. Julia was such an intelligent, pretty girl, somewhat shy and a very good kind friend, that could supply an objective answer to a dilemma.

"Julia, I need you to help me," Mary confided as soon as they were sitting alone on the front porch. She proceeded to tell her friend the conversation that took place while she was talking to her cousin George. What did she think of the response and was it wrong to break an engagement?

"That was a mistake to begin with Mary. I sensed from the start that Henry was much too quick to get serious. He put you in an awkward position when presenting you with a ring in front of an audience. You are right, the ring should be returned but do be gentle. He will be drafted soon and I'm sure you will find the right words when the opportune time arrives," Julia advised. The opportune time arrived the next evening. Henry phoned Mary at work and suggested they go out to dinner. It was Henry who brought up the topic of war and the draft. Surprisingly, Mary had little trouble convincing the young man that it was a bad time to plan marriage or even have a steady relationship with the future so uncertain.

Francis phoned from Malone early one Sunday morning. "I've been discharged from the Army. My legs have been giving me problems since I had a bout with pneumonia a few weeks ago. Irene and I will be in Rochester for a visit and I can give you details. I'm fine, so don't worry. It'll be a few weeks before I get everything settled here. I'LL be phoning often and keep you updated."

Josephine and the girls were at Mass when the call came in. Lorenzo relayed the news as soon as they returned from church. The father completed the account by expressing his feelings about the discharge. He turned to his wife and said,

"At least we know that Frank is safe. The boys needed to serve in the military. It is their country, but it is a dangerous time."

The eldest son phoned often and had long chats with each member of the family. Lorenzo became uneasy after several months passed and Francis made no move to come for a Rochester visit.

"I think we should go to Malone for a visit. Frank liked to come for visits to Rochester. I'll feel better if I know that he is fine," suggested the father.

The parents arrived in the North Country mid October on a Sunday afternoon. The fall foliage displayed an array of deep red, yellow and orange. An awesome sight! That late afternoon, when they drove up to Frank's home, the parents expected the young couple to be sitting on the front porch or at least in sight somewhere in the spacious beautiful front lawn. Not so. The door and windows were shut.

"They must be out," suggested Lorenzo.

After returning to the car for a short time, the parents got out of the auto and walked about the grounds. After a little while, a Ford drove up with Irene at the wheel and Frank sitting beside her. At first glance, seeing his father and mother, Francis gave a hearty welcome followed by smiles and greetings from Irene. Irene quickly got out of the car and opened the door to the house. Francis was taking a long time getting out of the automobile. Irene hurried back to help her husband. Shocked at what they witnessed, both parents were silent.

"You were injured, then," finally spoke up the father. "We wanted to surprise you. Are you well enough to have us around?" questioned the father.

"Of course and we are happy you are here. I look worse than what I feel. I have no pain," the son assured his worried parents. Lorenzo and Josephine remained the week. After a few days, both parents got used to the change in their son. He dragged his leg but continued to carry on. Irene shared her concerns with the mother while Frank and Lorenzo drove around the area afternoons.

"Mama, Frank does not like to be seen limping. When you arrived we had just returned from church. We no longer attend St. Mary's. Frank wants me to drive to a church where we are not recognized. He seldom leaves the house. I spoke to the doctor and he had a long talk with Frank. His doctor suggested that Frank must work at something. We no longer have the store, he sold the boat, too. He will be working as town clerk next week. He also signed up for refresher courses in engineering. I'm praying that he finally will get work that gives him back some dignity."

"You are a good wife. Keep encouraging him. God willing, he will come out of this without too much scarring," offered the concerned mother.

Other members of the family came for visits. Soon, Francis became accustomed to his disability. He was hired to be on the corps of engineers who would be working on the St. Lawrence Seaway. Once he was gainfully employed he was his old self.

Mary, too, visited the brother several times. Irene enjoyed driving around the mountainous region explaining some of the Indian folklore. She knew names and functions and medical value of wild plants and weeds. There was an Indian reservation not far from Malone. Irene's family was friendly with the folks on the reservations. The Tantalos enjoyed spending time in the North Country. There was so much to see.

When there was certainty that war would end. Lorenzo and his wife received word from the war department that Dom was indeed living but was a prisoner of war in Japan. The news was a relief. However, family members were concerned about the over all health of the young man.

A marriage that was put on hold soon took place. Nancy and her fiancé decided on a simple wedding.

Knowing that Francis Long's mother would still remain in residence in her new home, Nancy planned to continue her designing career. The new bride was happy that her mother-in-law would continue to run the house. Her husband assured her that she could continue with her career after marriage. Hats, and especially custom made head apparel, were in vogue. Frequently, Nancy went to New York City to select materials and examine the latest designs. Attending fashion shows were also part of the trip. Her sister Patricia was happy these trips would continue. Patricia and sometimes Pat Costa would accompany her.

Pat Costa was a frequent visitor at the Tantalo home.

Although the young woman was satisfied with her job as sales clerk, she had always dreamed of being a paid singer at some future date. One Saturday afternoon, she arrived at her friends' home close to tears.

"My career as singer must be abandoned," sobbed Pat. "My instructor at the Eastman School of Music told me that he is terminating my lessons after my three years of study. My last lesson will be in two months. He suggested I go to New York City for further study. There is no demand for my classical voice in the Rochester arena. Only popular singers are now in demand."

"Don't rush to any conclusion. After the two months, let's go to New York City and check it out. Nancy will still be making trips there. You like the big city and you have cousins there. That should be a comfort to you," encouraged her friend.

As Patricia predicted, her sister Nancy did continue trips to New York City as well as Buffalo. Of course the would be singer was invited to go along. The big city, New York, was Pat Costa's choice. She remained with relatives, found work in a department store and also found a voice teacher. After several years, however, the singer realized it was futile to continue music studies. She remained a sales lady until the time of her retirement.

"Arts, artists and musicians do not get sponsorship in America. Your father was right when he discouraged you from being an artist. So much of my meager weekly wages went to pay for voice lessons. From now on I am going to be contented to be in the church choir," confessed Pat to her friends Patricia and Nancy.

More furloughs were being given to the military. One day Mary received a phone call from her friend Helen and was told that she would be in town for several weeks.

"You look great in the uniform, Helen, and you have such a tan. The Army must agree with you," Mary complimented her friend when she came for a visit.

"Well, I like my work and I met such a nice fellow. He, too, works with me. I am engaged." With the statement, Helen showed her friend the ring on her finger. The two friends spent a long time getting caught up on what had transpired since their last get together.

"I can't believe that I have been in the army four years. Are you still working at Armour and do you still keep in touch with Henry?" questioned Helen of her friend.

"No, to both. I stopped writing to Henry. Our letters became shorter and we finally stopped exchanging letters.

Just after you left, I started to work for a much smaller company. It is also a food-distributing center. There are only five of us on the office staff. Four of the girls work in the outer office but I have my own cubbyhole. A friend of mine was leaving the accountant's job to join her husband in Washington. This work has more phases to it, I don't have to work Saturdays and I get a commission of all sales. The boss is great. He even allows me to smoke in my office. Two of the girls have husbands overseas. It's tough on them. One of them sobs every time she gets a letter from her husband. He is still in heavy combat I think. Do you think the war will ever end?" enquired Mary.

The response came quick and very decisively, "I'm sure it will be and it better be. A year from now will be my wedding date. We plan a fall wedding and, of course, you will be in the wedding party," joyfully responded the friend.

Helen's friend responded in a soft tone, "I may not be in Rochester next year. Although I am not sure yet, but I'm thinking of entering the convent. Please don't reveal this. We need some one in the family as a religious. Perry has already made plans to marry. If I'm entering I need to decide soon."

"I don't like that at all! When you are a nun you can't go and come as you please. We have been such good friends. I'll miss you very much," answered Mary's friend. The war lasted more than a year. Gerald, Helen's fiancé, had a minor injury in the war. The much-desired marriage did not take place until three years later.

After Helen returned to her Army base, months of inner conflicts overtook Mary's thoughts. She was searching for pros and cons of religious life. She repeatedly asked herself, "I may not be good enough to be a religious, I'll miss family and friends. What kind of work will I be given, I like my job. I'm sure I will not like wearing all those black clothes." These and other similar reflections occupied much of Mary's thinking.

An event took place at work that made Mary realize she could no longer be indecisive. An accountant from the main office examined account books once a year. The office staff where Mary worked was conscientious and valued accuracy. There was never a problem with the books during the five years Mary was the accountant. Company books were examined and the report was given to the staff at a company dinner following the scrutiny of the books.

At the end of the meal, the examiner made a very peculiar statement.

"Mary, let me look at your left hand. Oh, you are not engaged? That means you will not be leaving the company for a while. That's good news."

The next day Mary realized why he made the statement. Her boss, Mr. McQuiet, called her into his office. After congratulating her on the books' accuracy, she was asked,

"Are you willing to be trained as a traveling auditor for the company? You would be in training for about a year, then be responsible for the books of a region."

After a short reflection, Mary responded, "That would interest me and I'm sure the answer would be yes but I need to consider another option. Can I give you a definite answer after my vacation?"

Mary was having a two weeks vacation starting the following day. She immediately asked herself,

"Are you, or aren't you going to be a nun?"

Much had to be done during the following two weeks. What steps does one take to be a nun? She decided that she would follow Pauline's advice. Talk to a priest. She phoned the rectory and made an appointment to see Father Mooney the first day of her vacation. It was a lengthy discussion and he did encourage her to take the first steps.

"You will be given time to examine the life while you are a postulant. You will be a postulant for two years. Each order has it's own time line. Phone Sister Helen, she is the leader of the Sisters of St. Joseph here in Rochester. Or you can consider the cloistered order, the Carmelites.

"What's the difference?" questioned the young woman.

"Cloistered nuns are much stricter. The rule of silence is very demanding and in fact the rule involves rigorous discipline," informed the priest.

"I don't think I'll consider the cloister," said Mary.

12
Preparing to Take First Vows

With the local telephone directory open on the living room table, Mary was jotting down addresses to convents. Phone rings, however, did not interrupt her concentration. Her teenage sisters, Lucy and Amy were on vacation and were obsessed with phone calls. The two young girls were the first to answer phone rings. Other family members gave them full reign over the telephone.

"The phone call is for you, Mary," shouted Amy.

Impatient with the interruption, Mary picked up the phone and Julia was at the other end of the line.

"I'm at work. My cousin, Gigi, is coming for a visit and will be at the train station at 12 o'clock. Can you meet the Auburn train and entertain her until I get out of work? She just graduated from high school and will be visiting this week. Are you free to meet her?" pleaded Mary's friend.

"Of course, I'll be in the area soon and it will not be a problem," responded Mary.

"Well, that gives me little choice. Only four more vacation days. I still don't know the answers. Will I be going to a convent? If yes, what convent? Sister Helen is not available. So, I'll go to a close convent near the train station," Mary decided. Glancing at the recently compiled list she decided St. Joseph's Convent would be her first try.

Arriving in an area close to the train station, Saint Joseph's Convent and Business School was on a busy street not far from the city's Main Street. This was a familiar area, not far from Mary's former office and near the church she often visited when shopping. As she approached the Convent, however, the would be religious candidate became apprehensive. The building was well maintained but old. She rang the doorbell and was not anxious to encounter an unfamiliar nun. A young religious opened the huge door, and smilingly led her into a formal small parlor.

"What can I do for you," asked the young nun.

"I need information on religious life, what are the requirements and what programs are part of the training?"

The questions and phrases Mary used were direct quotes from Father Mooney's interview.

The young nun responded, "I'm not going to be much help. Those are questions that Sister Superior can answer. She is at a meeting right now. I'd suggest you return in about an hour. Can you do that?"

Reassured by such a pleasant encounter, Mary agreed to return after she met with Gigi at the train station. It was close to noon when she met Julia's cousin. The girls stopped at a nearby diner and after lunch, Gigi agreed to accompany Mary to the Convent.

As she rang the bell, Mary felt much more comfortable than she did earlier. Again, it was the young nun who answered the door. Smilingly, she led both girls to the familiar front parlor and told them to sit for a few minutes. She would announce their arrival. There was a large contrast between Gigi and Mary. The young traveler was simply dressed in white blouse, black loafers, white socks and was in a navy pleated skirt. Her face was devoid of make-up and she had a short simple haircut. It was quite evident that Gigi was a teenager.

There was no doubt the applicant for religious life, however, was a fashionable career woman. Her auburn hair had been freshly styled by a hairdresser. She wore a   tailored pink suit, matching accessories and high-heeled shoes. When the older nun, also smiling and pleasant, walked into the room directed her remarks to Gigi.

"I'll be happy to give you information about our congregation and the work we do. Here is a book on the foundress of our order." She handed the book to the girl.

"I'm just visiting Rochester. I do not plan to enter the convent. She is the one that needs the information," the shocked young girl quickly enlightened the nun. Sister Edward, the superior, faced Mary and with a surprised expression questioned,

"How old are you?"

"I just turned twenty-seven," Mary responded.

"You are still in the range of entrance. We do not admit women after they reach their 28th birthday. I can give you some literature. I'll be happy to answer any questions you may have." The Sister continued to smile and was friendly. It dispelled some of Mary's anxiety. It was a long visit and even Gigi asked questions. Sister Edward gave Mary some solid information.

Both girls received brochures, leaflets and Mary received several books to read. It was suggested the applicant report to the Convent every other week. Visits to the convent would give the woman an opportunity to meet with other sisters living at the convent and ask questions that needed to be answered. It was also suggested that Mary meet with her pastor, get a letter of approval and have a prayer program set up.

"Spend time at quiet prayer each day. Ask for God's blessing. I'll pray, too, and so will the Sisters. Do you mind handing me your purse?"

That was a strange request but the purse was given to the nun. Opening the purse and pointing to a pack of cigarettes, sister smilingly said, "You need to give these up if you become a Sister."

Both girls spent some time visiting the shops in the area and finally went to Julia's nearby office. Since the two cousins had plans for the evening, Mary was relieved to be alone. It was late afternoon and an ideal day to walk home.

"I'll stop at the rectory and check with Father Mooney. He will be able to advise me on what steps I should be taking." Reflecting on the convent visit, Mary began to feel more comfortable with the idea of becoming a nun. She was happy Father was in his office. Reporting on the recent convent visit was met with approval from the Pastor. Father Mooney suggested she tell her parents and employer. He also suggested making an appointment with Father O'Brien. He would be a good choice for spiritual director and could provide her with a daily prayer program. Father O'Brien was the young parish curate. The priest had the reputation of being an aesthetic prayerful man.

"I want to wait a year. Is that OK?" asked Mary.

"That is a good plan. You will have time to get used to the idea. You may have some problems getting used to Convent life. You are much too independent. I am familiar with the Sisters of Notre Dame, the order you are interested in. It is international and the motherhouse for this province is in Baltimore. That means you may be missioned away from Rochester. Their rule is also strict on enclosure. That means visits are restricted." The priest was giving Mary information to help her decide on the drawbacks of living convent life.

The young woman was suffering from information overload. She knew so little about nuns and convent life. Later, reflection on the choice, she realized that it would have made a difference in her selection of a congregation if she realized what strict enclosure meant.

When Mary returned to work after vacation she immediately gave her employer the answer to the job advancement.

"Mr. McQuiet, I'm tempted to accept the promotion offer but I must refuse. I plan to leave in about a year. However, I would like to remain in my present capacity. I am seriously considering becoming a nun. I may change my mind but right now I am at the consideration stage. Will that jeopardize my job?"

"No, certainly not. I would appreciate any time you can give. The girls in the outer office get   along well with you and it's a relief having a team that works well together. Although I am not a Catholic, I would never discourage a young person from following a religious calling."

Mary responded, "May I please ask a favor of you? I'd prefer you not mention my decision to the employees. I want to make sure that I am on firm ground before I make my decision known. My parents will know and a very few friends as well."

Within a few days after meeting with Sister Edward, Mary discussed religious life with her parents. They, too, agreed that it would not be mentioned until Mary had some very definite plans. The young woman began to realize the repercussions of her decision.

"A family is blessed if a child follows a religious calling. You are one of ten children, but each child is very important and loved. We shall miss you very much." The mother tearfully responded.

The father, however, was skeptical. "Do you realize holy vows are taken? They are very binding. You cannot compare them to an engagement or even a marriage vow. In some cases, dispensations must be acquired to leave the convent. Once you take vows, you remain in the assigned work."

The parents' reaction made the woman realize she would miss her family, worry about her mother and wondered if she could really live the new rigorous, unfamiliar life.

Despite changes in her life's journey, Mary adjusted without major problems. Her sister Patricia, occasionally would point out these changes. On one occasion, while both women were reading in the upstairs study, Pat asked,

"How come you haven't been smoking?"

"I've decided to stop smoking," was the quick response from the younger sister.

"I can't believe you are giving up cigarettes without a serious reason. Every time I suggested you give them up for Lent you refused. Did the doctor tell you to quit?"

"Of course not, I just changed my mind." Pat, puzzled, shrugged her shoulders and continued reading without further comment.

Mary was an addicted reader. She often returned from the library with an arm full of books. Her selections included recent publications and especially mysteries. She began restricting her trips to the library but did have a large collection of spiritual books on the bookshelf. Most of the titles were books borrowed from St. Joseph's Convent library or books from St. Patrick's rectory collection. Again Patricia noticed something was different.

"How come you are reading all spiritual books? What happened to mysteries?"

"So I'm changing reading habits. No big deal," Mary responded.

Days, weeks and even months were fast melting away. As the time of leaving began to approach, Mary began reflecting,

"I'm going to miss thanksgiving celebrations. What will Christmas be like at the convent? I'm sure it will not only be different, but also not to my liking." These and similar musings passed through the young woman's mind.

Mary paid regular visits to the convent. Sister Edward and the other sisters at St. Joseph answered questions, offered suggestions and helped her get clothing that she would be wearing as a candidate. Candidate, was the term sisters used for a woman planning an introduction to entering a convent. Occasionally, the girl's cousin Perry would accompany her to the Convent for visits. Mary also visited the rectory and met with Father O'Brien. They would discuss the prayer program or scripture readings.

Shortly after Nancy's wedding, all five of the Tantalo girls were invited to visit the newly decorated bride's home.

It was only a few weeks before Mary's entrance date to the convent. The young woman decided it would be a good time to inform her sisters of the decision to become a nun. After lunch, while all were gathered in Nancy's living room, Mary gave them the news.

"You can't be serious?" questioned Francis, the eldest sister.

"How can you decide on such a change in your life? You never attended Catholic schools, don't know sisters and besides, some of them can be pretty bossy," offered Nancy.

"Oh, don't go," spoke up a tearful Lucy.

"No wonder you gave up smoking. I hate nun's clothing. Their shoes are heavy and they are wrapped in so much material." Patricia added.

"I don't think you should go," spoke Amy the youngest.

It was a very uncomfortable time for Mary. None of her sisters liked her choice. Josephine discussed convent life with her daughters. The mother, of course, stressed the spiritual advantages and they all got used to the idea. Father Mooney had stopped in one evening to visit Lorenzo. He brought up the subject in the presence of all the girls. His point of view and input made the idea more tolerable. He explained that candidates were given at least two years training initially. Also several more years of direction and active service would precede the taking of final vows. Young women were free to leave the convent if they were candidates or had not taken final vows.

August twenty-fifth was the day of departure for the Baltimore motherhouse Convent. Mary arrived at the Rochester convent early morning to prepare for the ceremony and change into the garb of a candidate. When she arrived at the Rochester convent, she was assigned a visitor's room for the day. After examining the clothing that had been compiled, she changed into the candidate's garb. The dress was no problem. It was similar to the academy's black uniform with white collar and cuffs. However, it was a long version and reached the top of her shoes. Black cotton stockings, heavy black oxfords and short cape were bearable but a white stiff bonnet was much too large and clumsy. Frowning to herself, she thought,

"Well, Pat did warn me about the clothing!"

All family members were gathered in the front parlor and as Mary entered, Amy said,

"You look nice. Don't worry about the clothing."

"Are you too warm?" questioned the mother.

"No, I'm fine," with that, the smiling daughter sat next to her mother. Mary greeted Frank and Irene who had come to be with the family.

"We are driving you to the train station after the ceremony," the brother offered.

The service was short. Family members were invited into

the dining room for refreshments at the end of the service. Lorenzo seemed uncomfortable and fidgety. He was always careful not to show his emotions when he became worried. Similarly, when the sons came home for a short furlough, he never prolonged departures.

"We had better be leaving, Frank, we don't want to be late for boarding the train. Sister Edward and another sister will meet us there. They have already left," suggest the father.

Another candidate, Veronica, from St. Michaels's parish was also going to be met at the station. Irene and Mary sat at the back seat and Lorenzo offered to drive. Francis didn't argue but sat at the front passenger seat while the father sat at the wheel and drove silently. Mid way he asked,

"What is the work of the congregation?" asked the father.

"It is a teaching order but I don't know what my assignment will be," the daughter answered.

"Ask for a teaching assignment. There are many educators in the family. Your grandmother worked with Dr. Montessori devising methods of teaching," suggested the father.

The two young women were sitting together in the back seat. Irene whispered softly to her sister in law. "Your father is happy about that. He wants teachers in the family."

Two sisters and a candidate were waiting for Lorenzo's daughter. The father reminded the girl that if she was unhappy she should phone and one of them would be happy to drive her back home. Irene handed Mary a box of Fanny Farmer's candy as the group left the waiting religious at the train station. Both candidates followed the two nuns boarding the train.

The group of religious sat on the side seats of the train. It was a hot ride that August day. Mary handed the box of candy to one of the nuns. The opened box was passed to the other three women. Veronica sullenly refused the treat. Although

Mary was apprehensive and concerned about her new home, she was anxious for the trip to end.

"Train stations are always dirty, hot and noisy," thought Mary when they arrived. Turning to the young candidates, Sister Edward instructed, "Just follow us, we will lead the way." There was no lingering. Outside the station two waiting nuns, standing next to a large car, smilingly greeted the group. All hurried into the car driven by Henry, the jack of all skills maintenance man for the motherhouse.

As soon as pleasantries were exchanged, the nuns from Baltimore took out two sheets of paper.

"Good, you have the list of changes. Read the list," said Sister Edward. Sister Carmel began citing the names of nuns, where they had been stationed and the new assigned convent and grade change. The list included all grade levels assignments as well as cities in states along the United States eastern seaboard. There were also some sisters being sent to Puerto Rico. At the end of the reading, Sister Edward took out a similar listing and also read assignment changes. From time to time there would be a comment from one of the nuns,

"That nun needed a change. We all know that she could not teach boys' classes.

She is too soft spoken. Good she went to the all girls' school." Such comments interrupted the readings.

"Wow, that's what Father Mooney meant. I can be sent Lord knows where," thought Mary.

Henry stopped the car in front of a large gate, the entrance to the candidates' new home. It was a large brick well maintained building on a crowded, noisy city street. Unlike the building they were entering, the structures across the street seemed neglected and dirty. The front door opened into a small entry way and a few wide steps. Without delay, they were in a large room that included several entrances to other sections of the building. One was the school entrance. Following the lead of the nuns, the candidates were ushered through another door into a wide bright hallway with highly polished linoleum floors. Walls were decorated with framed calligraphic sayings and proverbs. Some were fine stitched lovely pieces of needlework.

Offices lined the wide corridor. An open door revealed a large office and a few inner offices. The two candidates were led into a small simple furnished office. Sister Patricia was sitting at the desk, receptionist for the Provincial Superior. She smiled and warmly greeted to two Rochester sisters that had traveled with the young women.

"How is the cold country," she laughingly welcomed the group.

Addressing Sister Edward, Sister Patricia added, "Will you be staying in Baltimore for a while?"

"No, we will remain a day or two. School will be starting and we do need to prepare for classes."

"Let's introduce these young women to the candidature and the director can get them settled before you are ready to return to Rochester. You may want to see them again before you leave." Continued Sister Patricia.

The young women were led to a wide slate stairway. Highly polished banisters were gripped as the two candidates mounted the stairway that led them to another wide hall. Classrooms lined the corridor. At the end of the hall a large room could be seen. Mary saw a group of young women, dressed much like herself and Veronica. They were laughing and conversing.

Although the girls were led toward the large room, they were escorted into an adjacent small office. Two sisters, standing by the window, turned as they heard St. Patricia's greeting. Sister Ann addressed them,

"Welcome! Thank you sisters, you can leave Mary and Veronica. I'm sure they are hungry and tired. Let them have a good meal, rest and get acquainted with the other candidates." Turning to Sister Edward, the sister continued, "Stop in tomorrow before you leave."

Sister Ann was a small elderly nun and the one beside her seemed very young but also tiny.

"This is Sister Madeline and I'm Sister Ann. We are here to help you. We are having free days until early September. Sister Madeline will give you a start and show you around. We meet in the candidature each evening at eight p.m. You will be given information along with the other girls. We refer to you as first year candidates. There will be about fifty women in your group. The second year candidates' group is smaller. There are only thirty-eight of them. Each candidate is assigned a companion. We refer to them as angels. They are truly angels because they are a great help to newcomers."

Orders were then given to Sister Madeline. "Show them their places in the dormitory. They can deposit their luggage. Then take them to the refectory and they will be served supper. When they are rested, introduce them to the other candidates and their assigned angels. Candidates, I'll see you again for instruction at eight o'clock."

Sister Madeline was friendly, talkative and both girls seemed more relaxed. She led them up a flight of stairs to the dorms.

"You will both be in short dorm. There are about twenty girls in this section."

There were two rows of white beds. White heavy material dividers surrounded each section. Next to the bed there was a nightstand. On top of each stand Mary noticed a large china basin and pitcher. The nun kept referring to each section as a cell.

"This is your cell, Mary. Veronica, you are at the end of this row."

"May I remove my bonnet?" asked Veronica as she headed toward her cell.

"Oh, of course, Mary you take yours off too. I'll take the bonnets. The only time you wear them is when you go to chapel for Mass or you need to go out. They are clumsy. I'll leave you here to get cleaned up and unpack. The toilets and showers are at the other end of the dorm. I'll be back in twenty minutes. That will give the kitchen time to get a meal ready for you," offered the sister.

The girls busied themselves with unpacking. There wasn't much room in their bed stands. No wonder Sister Edward kept telling Mary that there was little storage space at the motherhouse. Supplies and additional items would be stored in their trunks. As Mary went to investigate the location of bathrooms she passed a large room. There were rows of trunks lined against the walls. Large Names were printed on each trunk.

"This must be the trunk room," thought Mary.

As Mary was returning to her cell, Veronica met her.

The girl seemed different. With a warm smile, she confessed, "That bonnet was killing me. It was much too small for me. I thought I would never get it off my head. Yours was much too big for you. I was going to ask you to trade with me but I was feeling too miserable."

The two women were getting acquainted when Sister Madeline interrupted,

"The food is ready for you. I'll take you to the refectory.

After your meal I'll introduce you to your angels and they will be happy to show you around."

While the two girls were eating, Veronica told Mary that she was quite familiar with religious life. She went to high school at the Notre Dame's boarding academy. In fact, she knew who her angel was going to be.

"I'm sure Vera will be my angel. She went to the academy and is a second year candidate. We were good friends in high school and she has been writing me letters," Veronica said. The girls continued their get acquainted conversation and after a short time were interrupted by two lively girls. Veronica hugged a tall blond girl. A dark-haired girl greeted Mary.

"I'm Jackie. I'll be your angel and hope you will be happy here. We are free for two more hours. That will give us some time to examine the motherhouse and I can also tell you what the other girls learned last night. You and Veronica are the last to arrive."

Jackie was an attractive slim young woman with a braid coiled around her head.

"I like your hair do," said Mary.

"Many of us wear this hair style. Of course we may not go to hair salons. All are encouraged to wear a simple hair- style. It makes sense you know. We will be taking a vow of poverty. Besides, nuns wear their hair very short under the veil. My aunt is a nun. She tells me a lot about the rules." Jackie was feeding the young candidate as much information as she could before it would be time for instruction. After the two newcomers were given a tour of the motherhouse and introduced to other members, they were invited to go for a snack.

Finally the girls went along with all the other candidates in to the big candidature. The room resembled a very large classroom. Rows of desks were quickly being occupied with the young women. Mary and Veronica were led to their assigned places.

Sister Ann walked into the room and at exactly eight o'clock, a small desk bell was rung. At the sound of the bell, chatting stopped, then all the women stood and a few familiar prayers were recited. At the end of prayer, Sister Ann invited the two new candidates to stand. They were introduced to the large group and all the girls gave a cheery WELCOME then clapped their hands. Mary was happy that she was not the only one being introduced. Each evening, the young women were given guidelines. Instructions were informal and covered such topics as schedules, programs, activities and other pertinent topics. The young women spent the next two weeks getting acquainted with each other and being interviewed for program initiation.

The director of education and Sister Ann set up programs or suggested teaching assignments. Women that had degrees prior to entrance, were often given part time teaching responsibilities in the nearby Baltimore schools. Both nuns were in the office for Mary's first interview.

"We have examined your education records and also received a letter of commendation from your employer. Our first program choice was a teaching assignment and a one year candidature. Sister Rose, however, feels that you should have a two-year term. You need educational courses especially if you go on to further study. We are a teaching congregation. Some of our schools require a masters degree. Spending two years at study will also include religion courses. You did not attend Catholic schools. A strong understanding of the Catholic faith is necessary if you are to make the correct vocation choice. Your decision to become a nun must be made after you have spent a year as novice, said Sister Ann.

Two years of study and prayer ended quickly. Aside from exchange of letters, there was little contact with family and friends. Candidates, however, were allowed a two week home visit the Christmas before becoming novices.

"Sister Ann will give you some do and don't commands before you leave for your home visit," warned some of the senior candidates. Sure enough, long talk preceded the day before the candidates left for their journeys.

"Candidates, remember that this is one of the last visits you make to your family. This is a semi-cloistered order. Our rule allows few visits. Family visits are permitted only for funerals of each parent and two more visits during the serious illness of parents. This visit is for your parents and therefore you are to be at their service during the time at home. Help where you can and remember you are a nun in training. Deport yourself properly, your prayer schedule should be adhered to and take along a spiritual book for reading. All your time must be spent with your parents. Visiting friends, shopping, going to movies or restaurants are not to be part of your visit.

You have spent almost two years living the life of a religious. Some days may have been difficult for you. Much depended on your ability to adjust to the rigorous training and study. The novitiate and religious life under vows will not be easier. Please reflect on your future as a Catholic sister very carefully. This is the best time to objectively decide if you can live a vowed life. You may remain at home if you so desire. When you arrive home contact a Sister of Notre Dame living in your town. If you have any problems, have needs or decide religious life is not for you, that sister can advise you. Enjoy your visit and I hope you all return," was the warm farewell from Sister Ann.

Heavy snowdrifts were swirling around the two Rochester girls, Mary and Veronica, as they left the train station to meet family members. Outdoor-wear for the Notre Dame Candidate included a heavy black cape and bonnet. Both women enjoyed being with family and often phoned each other during the visit. They both chose to return to the convent despite the difficult separation from family.

Several weeks after Mary returned from her home visit, preparations were being made to enter the Novitiate. This would be a year of contemplation, silence and preparation for two contemporary vow terms. Final vows followed two three-year terms. Mary's year as Novice proved to be one of the most tranquil and peaceful times. The Novices met often to chant, sing, and study the teaching's of the Church. Blocks of time were allotted for private prayer and visits to the chapel.

13
Living the Semi Cloistered Life as an Educator

Four of the newly temporary vowed nuns were strolling along the tree-lined path of the novitiate. Wearing newly received black veils, all were discussing their new assignments. Most of them would be traveling the next day.

"I am assigned to Brooklyn. When the novice director asked if I would like to teach at an Italian Parish School, I assured her I would be delighted. I thought I would be sent to Rochester, my home town," said Mary.

"You still have a lot to learn. Good thing you still have more time before final vows. First of all, we have no schools in Rochester that are connected to the Italian Parishes. Most of our schools in the cold city are St. Michael, Holy Family and Holy Redeemer. They all are in German neighborhoods. Further more, rarely is a newly professed sent to her home town." Veronica informed the listening group.

"Oh, I am going to Brooklyn, too," happily joined in Mildred, the youngest of the group.

Indeed, the two were going to the same school and were assigned middle grades. Mary, although disappointed that she would not be close to family, thought it was nice to have one from the group as a colleague. Several teachers were going to Florida and three were being sent to Puerto Rico.

Mary had packed and was ready for the next day's departure. It was a hot early afternoon and she found a bench close to a cool shady spot. As she sat comfortably, gazing at the beauty of the large, luxuriant lush vegetation of the grounds, she mused,

"I will miss my long prayer times of this canonical year.

This is a strange feeling. All of a sudden, I am homesick. It was great the family came from Rochester for the vow ceremony. Mama looked so elegant in her new striped navy suit with delicate white blouse. There was some activity in chapel during the ceremony. I was afraid it was Mama. Her respiratory illness always causes her discomfort when she is in a crowded place. Lucy is such a pretty girl and Papa was so quiet. He thinks I wont like being a nun. Strange that he seemed to want me to like religious life but did offer me a way out."

Visiting day, Lorenzo took Mary aside.

"I want you to keep in mind that if you feel convent life is not for you, leave. There is a fund laid aside for your use. It is a trust for you and in Lucy's name. The family knows of the account and all agree that it's a bad thing to be a religious if the life is too difficult."

When the Tantalo boys were in the service, they were never given news that would worry or distress them. Similarly, this was also true now that Mary was in the convent. Unknown to her daughter in the convent, Josephine had a few very weak spells prior to her visit to Baltimore for the religious ceremony. However, a few weeks before the date of travel, she had improved dramatically.

It was very hot and humid that August day when Mary's mother was in chapel to witness the taking of vows. Shortly before the end of the service, when Josephine had a coughing and weak spell, one of the nuns escorted the family out of chapel and took them to a cool library reading room. The comfortable cool space, a cool fruit drink and quiet time helped significantly. One of the professed nuns met Josephine's daughter after the services and led her to the library. The newly professed was greeted with smiles, tears and emotion. Three years had passed since she last saw members of the family.

Reflecting on the family visit on vow day, Mary again began to feel the disappointment of not being sent closer to her home.

"I should know better than expect to go to Rochester. That wouldn't help. Home visits are not permitted and family members may visit only one afternoon a month. Big deal!

Gosh, I'm certainly a lot older than most of the girls in my group. They are so young and not only understood what they were giving up, but also are ready to do God's work. Get on with it," Mary chastised herself. Alone, and quickly wiping the streaming tears, the young woman slipped into the convent chapel unnoticed and prayed.

Excitement was at a high level the day of departure from the novitiate. Mary as well as a large group of nuns was ready to leave very early in the morning. Sisters of Notre Dame did not drive in the mid nineteen hundreds. Friends and family members usually chauffeured them to destinations. When the departure time arrived for each sister or group of sisters, the names were called out and they were taken to train stations. Mary and Mildred were with the last group to leave. Restlessness had taken over at such a long wait. Both girls were silent as they were being driven to the station.

"We will probably be left off in New York City. I'm sure there will be two nuns waiting for us," said Mildred. Mary realized that her companion knew much more about convent life than she did. Mildred also had attended the Notre Dame Academy. Sure enough, nuns did meet them, but not two, there were four of them. Two of them were waiting for four other sisters having New York City assignments. After some discussion, Mary and Mildred were instructed to sit on one of the benches while phone calls were being made.

Mary's companion felt faint.

"It's almost six hours since our last meal. Lets see what our bag of goodies contains. You should eat something," suggested Mary.

The bag contained small tuna sandwiches and two bananas. Both girls laughingly devoured the complete contents of the bag. Mildred was laughing and biting a cookie when two nuns returned. The girls were quickly directed to follow the two nuns. They would be boarding a subway car. When they arrived at the subway platform, Mary became terrified at the sight of so many cars speeding by. Large droves of people were rushing to get on. The three other nuns apparently were used to this mode of travel.

Breathlessly looking around her as she mounted the car, many passengers were standing holding on to straps. Mildred immediately grabbed a strap and handed it to Mary, then rushed to grab one for herself. The rest of the trip was a blur for Mary. All she remembered was rushing from one car to another. All four nuns arrived at the large convent, similar to the one in Rochester. Their new home was a brick structure on a busy street. The school was next to the convent and there was a church across the street.

After a quick introduction of the newly professed to the sisters at St. Jude's, the traveling companions left. There was a warm reception for the new arrivals. Fifteen sisters made up the group of nuns that served the parish. Sister Vincent, also a recently professed, helped them with their luggage and showed them the room they would occupy.

Surprisingly, it was a dorm. There were three beds with heavy white material separating the room into three quite large compartments. Each compartment had a bed, chair, a big wardrobe and a six-drawer bureau.

"The three of us will share this room. My quarters are next to the window." Sister Vincent informed them.

Mildred was already next to the center bed and quickly placed her suitcase on the bed. Mary would be next to the outside door. She liked that. Both girls were unpacking when the sister superior came into the room. The title, Sister Superior was the term used for a community leader prior to the changes brought about by the Second Vatican Council.

"Welcome, sisters, we are thankful that you have joined us. Leave your unpacking for later, freshen up and do come into the community room. We have some refreshments ready for us to enjoy. You need time to relax before our evening meal."

The warmth, concern and kindness of the charge sister endeared her to the new nuns. Both new comers liked the group of friendly and lively sisters. Although the close proximity of their rooms to the bustling, noisy city street, Mary slept very soundly.

"School starts later this fall. Good thing, it will give you almost two weeks to get your classrooms decorated and begin preparation for classes. I am going to work on my room this afternoon. Come with me and I'll get both of you started," offered Sister Vincent. Almost a whole week quickly vanished before Mary was satisfied with the appearance of her room. Sister Mildred had the classroom next to her. The girls were happy that they were working close by.

Afternoons of the preparation days were spent studying textbooks; manuals and learning to write weekly plan books. Sister Donna and Alice, the two junior high-grade teachers, instructed the new teachers. When sisters were not working in school doing chores around the convent, their base was the community room. This was a large room, usually on the main floor of the convent. Bookshelves and cupboards lined the walls. Each sister had a desk in this room. In most convents, nuns sat according to date of profession. Sister superior and the older sisters sat in the front, the younger ones at the end of the room.

"My children seem so little," thought Mary as she watched her class march into their new classroom.

Following the instructions given by Sisters Donna and Alice on class management, Mary's class followed all the directions given by the new teacher. The children were seated in alphabetical order. "Easier to memorize your class of forty or fifty if they are seated in a given arrangement to follow." advised Sister Donna. Both nuns, Sister Mary and Sister Mildred became fond of the young children at St. Jude's. Both had large classes by usual standards but with careful preparation, the program of study was well covered.

"Mildred, does the principal come and sit in the classroom afternoons?" question Mary after the first week of school.

"Yes, Sister Vincent told me that she visits classrooms often. New teachers are supervised regularly and get reports on teaching, subject content and class management. You don't have to worry. I heard Sister Madonna, the principal, tell Sister Vincent that we are doing very well," answered Mildred.

Sister Vincent often enlightened the new teachers when they met during recreation times. Some immediate bits of information included procedures, customs, and Notre Dame rule explanations. The new sisters learned something new each day. Superiors are often not only administrators of convents but they are also principals of the schools. Sister Madonna was not only principal but was also supervisor of all Notre Dame schools in the New York Diocese.

"We don't refer to Notre Dame Sisters as nuns but as sisters. Furthermore, a sister is addressed as Sister Mildred, Sister Mary, etc. I made the mistake when I came by using just first names and sometimes nicknames. Most of our time is spent in the community room or chapel. Usually, very little time is spent in our bedrooms. Your bedroom is only for sleeping.

After evening recreation, usually about an hour, we sit in the community room and prepare lessons, correct papers, etc. Too much talking is not allowed unless it is a holiday. After night prayer we keep complete silence until after breakfast. Of course, if it is necessary to give messages or help someone, it is permitted." Sister Vincent frequently gave additional information to the new teachers. The three, Sisters Mary, Mildred and Vincent were enthusiastic teachers, enjoyed their classes and often shared concerns, joys and classroom experiences.

On one occasion, while students were outdoors playing, Sister Mildred as well as Sister Mary noticed the harshness with which one of the sisters corrected the young students. Sharing this concern with Sister Vincent, they were told, "I'm not surprised, and Sister Mary Donald has been warned. She has tamed down quite a bit. Did you know that the pastor has asked for her transfer?"

"But she is still teaching here," questioned Mildred.

"This is her second year at St. Jude's. This is a trial year for her. She is to take final vows in August. I'm sure she will transfer or leave." Sister Vincent enlightened the two teachers.

When several other like incidents occurred, Sister Madonna told Sister Donald to remain at the convent for the rest of the week. The principal was going to cover her class.

The principal called for a brief meeting at school a few days later. Sister Donald came to school for the meeting. Sister Madonna explained that several items needed to be clarified and therefore, the monthly faculty meeting was held early. The principal explained several calendar changes, reminders of report due dates and then surprised the group.

"Like every profession, certain talents and disciplines are needed for careers. Teaching is a profession that calls for close relationships. Unless one has strong communication skills, teaching will be very stressful, ineffective and can also be damaging to the student as well as the teacher. There are times that a trial period is needed. No shame should ensue. If that is recognized early, it is a great blessing. It is a learning experience and then time to seek another path to serve.

Sister Donald is a good, prayerful woman. She has tried the teaching profession and finds her talents are not in the teaching field. We are happy that she will be leaving to study health services. This has been an ongoing discussion."

Each faculty member took time to meet with Sister Donald, congratulate her on the new career choice and promised to pray for her success.

"Teaching is fascinating and rewarding. Parents are so grateful for the slightest improvement in their children. All the teachers at St. Jude's seem to enjoy their classes and the children are happy," reflected Mary one evening as she was preparing the next day's lessons. Several happy months followed before she received a letter from her friend Julia.

The letter gave all the news on friends, work, activities and the last two paragraphs of the letter startled Mary. Julia had spent the evening visiting Josephine at the hospital. Mary had received a letter from her sister Patricia and there was no mention of the mother's illness. Sister Madonna approached the tearful sister and suggested,

"Phone your family. I know you got some bad news but your father phoned me today and said that your mother had surgery over a week ago. She is doing well and will be returning home in a few days."

Patricia answered the phone.

"Mary, I know what you are going to ask. Mama is fine. She needed surgery and did very well. We didn't want to worry you. You are so far away and would be upset especially if you did not get the doctor's prognosis right away," the sister reassured.

After the phone call, the principal discussed illness with the new sister.

"I had a long talk with your father. It is recommended that when there is a serious illness in the family the religious should be told. The sisters will offer prayers and if it is serious, a home visit can be recommended. The doctors are confident your mother is on the road to recovery. Should she or any other family member become ill, they will phone." The superior was not only comforting but convincing.

Summers were spent studying, working towards advanced degrees or teaching summer school. Sisters Mary and Mildred were to continue with studies. In the fall both felt like experienced teachers and were enthusiastically looking forward to the new school year.

Sister Mary received several letters from her sister Amy, the youngest member of the family. A fall wedding was being planned. Of course, Sister Mary would not be at the wedding. What a surprise, when shortly after the wedding date, Amy and her new husband came for a visit. They were a handsome couple and eager to make the most of the visit. Here was the baby all grown up, a Para legal and seemed so happy and joyful. Her husband was interested in photography and brought along a camera loaded with film.

"We may not have our pictures taken," responded Mary.

The pastor was in the church when Sister Mary was taking the couple on a tour of the buildings. After the introductions, Amy spoke up,

"I wish we could take some pictures to show my mother. Their rule does not allow picture taking," Amy informed the priest.

"She is no longer a novice. Take as many pictures as you like. If there is a problem, Sister Mary, I'll tell Sister Superior that it was my idea. I'm sure you have nothing to worry on that score."

Many pictures were taken and when the young bride wrote again, she told her sister to rejoice. The mother was delighted and happy that she had pictures. At the end of the day, sleep came quickly and Sister Mary slept soundly. There were very few gaps in a convent day. A bell sounded several times during the day. A five o'clock bell announced the start of a new day. Morning prayer, meditation and Mass followed and shortly after breakfast, eaten in silence, each sister went about chores and then to the start of the school day. Saturdays included a longer sleep with the rising bell usually rung at six-thirty. Saturdays were spent cleaning, taking turns in the laundry and the remaining time was used for personal responsibilities. Sunday was a quiet day of prayer and study.

It was on one of those quiet Sunday afternoons that Sister Mary was beckoned into the superior's office. She was told that her mother had a very weak spell. Doctor Flynn suggested Sister Mary be informed.

"Your mother is not well. I'm not only passing the information on to you but I also sent for train tickets. We will be leaving for Rochester and board the four o'clock train. You may not travel alone and I shall accompany you. During your visit, I shall be visiting our schools while you are staying with family," Sister Madonna recommended.

Immediately on arrival in Rochester, the two sisters hailed a cab and went directly to the hospital. Most of the family members were there. Josephine was so still and white. Patricia said,

"Tell mama that you are here. The doctor assured us she is aware of us."

After greeting the mother, the young sister sat next to the two youngest children. Lucy and Amy were holding rosaries and whispering prayers. Patricia suggested they return home to rest but both girls insisted on staying.

Sister Mary as well as Sister Madonna would be staying at a convent near the hospital. A car would be picking her up at nine that evening. The superior of St. Mary's convent told Mary that although sisters were not permitted to stay out after seven in the evening, she was given permission to remain later. Duration of a family visits was three days. When Sister Mary left the hospital on the fourth day, her mother's condition had not changed. Before she left, Dr. Flynn said,

"Your mother may come out of this. This is not her first bad spell and she may rally. Sorry your visit is so short."

The train ride to New York was a quiet one. The superior felt bad that the visit could not be extended. It was such a heartbreaking scene that ended the home visit. Sisters Donna and Alice were waiting at the train station.

With the warm greeting, the sisters told Sister Mary the sisters at the convent were continuing their praying for the family as well as the mother. The next day, when Sister Mary came into the schoolroom, her students greeted her warmly and told her that they were sorry her mother was ill. Many approached her during lunchtime as well as during recess. All assured her that they would be praying for her mother. That evening Sister reflected on the home situation and recalled the warmth of her students. Tears flowed along with her prayers.

"This is tough, others in the family are going to become ill, too. I'll not be able to visit. I don't know if I can handle this kind of situation. I don't miss the nice clothes, my own bedroom, dancing and all that other stuff, but this is far too hard for me," thought the new religious. Days were taken up with teaching, lesson preparation and study. Nights, however, were filled with doubts, worry and tears.

Several days later Alice came into her classroom after the students had been dismissed. The older nun had been reflecting on her own family's sicknesses and deaths. She sympathized with this new sister.

"Sister Mary, you are feeling rotten. You are so far away from family. Imagination always pictures the gloomiest side of our sacrifices. The biggest deprivation is not being present to family and friends when they are in need. We do have something powerful though, our faith and prayers.

The death of my parents and the loss of my two brothers in the war, were terrible. My sisters were both working but close to family. They had a dreadful time being present to family. Their own husbands and children made demands, too. At least we are here praying for family members, our paths are holy journeys and that is always consoling to family members," reassured Sister Alice.

At the time, it was no comfort for Sister Mary. She was still numb from the encounter at the hospital. Gradually, however, although the numbness was there, the students' needs seemed to overtake much of her thinking. Occasionally, she reflected on Sister Alice's words and her prayers were much more focused. God had gifted her with such beautiful memories of family. Memories would always be there for comfort.

Phone calls soon followed her visit. Her mother had been dismissed from the hospital.

"Mama is home now. A few days ago mother began eating well and Dr. Flynn is very pleased with her recovery. Lucy was upset the day after you left. Papa hired a private nurse to be with our mother when we were not able to be at the hospital.

After work, as Lucy walked into the room, the nurse was reading the paper and eating candy from a Fanny Farmer's box. Mama's room had not been cleaned and the food tray was still on the table. Lucy just up and fired the nurse.

She quit her job to take care of Mama. Dr. Flynn applauded her decision. She is doing a wonderful job taking care of mama. Dr. Flynn advised her to train for nursing but Lucy told him she would nurse only for a family member. He was really serious and thinks she is great." Pat assured the nun.

Periodical phone calls with direct conversations with the mother eased the situation. Conversations always had a happy tone with joyful messages and bits of good news.

Close to the end of the school year, Sister Madonna and several other superiors received a plea from the Provincial. She needed sisters to help in the health care center of the Baltimore motherhouse during the summer months.

"Do you have sisters that are willing to delay their studies for one year and offer the time for service? They will resume studies next year." The message was read to the teachers one evening.

Sister Mary volunteered to help out. The week before the end of the school year Mary received a phone call from her brother Fred.

"Mama died in her sleep this morning." The message was shocking! Numbly, Sister Mary told Sister Madonna and preparations were made for a home visit. Again, the superior took care of the details. Travel to Rochester, the wake, funeral and the return trip to the convent were covered in three days. Those three days were a blur for the daughter.

While the teachers at St. Jude's School were completing reports and getting ready for summer assignments, Mary was packing to spend the summer at the health care center in Baltimore. The center was referred to as Notch Cliff. When she arrived, a young nursing sister took the teaching sister on a tour. It was a picturesque sturdy stone structure. Fruit trees, pines and patches of vegetable fields surrounded the building. Amazed at the sight, Sister Mary questioned the nurse, Sister Georgina,

"I can see that there are rooms for the sick and the building is large. What puzzles me are all the small orchards and fields that are included here. It looks like a farm."

"Well, it's both. A place for our sick and aging sisters but also farm land. Vegetables and fruit grown here, supply the motherhouse and some of our convents. Retired sisters do most of the farm work."

The summer volunteer was introduced to the head nurse, Sister Charles. She was a native of Rochester and questioned,

"What parish did you come from and where did you live?"

Sister Charles then confided, "I am a convert to Catholicism. Most members of my family are Lutherans but we do have Catholic members in our family. My conversion was acceptable but when I decided to become a religious, my parents and other members of the family would not give consent. I waited until I was a nurse, over twenty-one and then decided to enter. It has always bothered me that I could not get my family's acceptance of the choice I made.

The summer volunteer was given clerical work to do in the medical library. The provincial, visiting Notch Cliff prior to the arrival of summer volunteers met with Sister Charles, informing her on the qualifications of each of the new comers.

"I suggest that Sister Mary not work directly with the sick. There has been a recent death in the family."

It was a different experience for Sister Mary. She met many women on the medical staff and other young sisters.

Summer volunteers came from different states. Evenings were free and spent outdoors. Conversations created a rich exchange of experiences. The luxurious vegetation, and warm nights afforded a beautiful setting for night prayers and song.

"You are having visitors this afternoon, sister Mary," announced Sister Charles the last day of Mary's service.

Lorenzo was driven to Baltimore by his son Francis and daughter in-in-law Irene. It was such a pleasant surprise. After a tour about the grounds and building, Sister Charles came to the front parlor and invited them to remain for the evening meal. The head nurse and Lorenzo were discussing Rochester and surprisingly, Sister Charles was related to the Tantalo's family lawyer and friend. After a lengthy conversation on family, Sister Charles spoke of a large donation made to the congregation by an anonymous donor in memory of her parents.

"I don't know who sent it," she said.

"I can ask Charles, that's your nephew, if you like," suggested Lorenzo.

"No, I'll just rest with their decisions. You can remember me to all of them but let them make the move," said the sister.

On leaving that evening, Mary's father said, "Its sad that the head nurse's family does not get in touch with her. I'm sure their feelings have changed after all these years."

A few days before the volunteers were to leave, the provincial phoned Sister Charles.

"I need a sister for a vacancy in a Puerto Rican school. Can you suggest a sister among the volunteers that could be assigned there?" asked the provincial.

"Sister Mary seems to adjust quickly to situations. Perhaps you can consider her," offered the head nurse.

The provincial acted on the suggestion. Sister Mary was not aware of her transfer until she returned to Brooklyn.

Excited over the new school year, all three of the younger sisters, Sisters Mildred, Mary and Vincent were on the way to decorate their classrooms. Sister Madonna stopped them and said,

"You are being transferred, Sister Mary. I am so sorry and the class you were given will be disappointed. A sister is needed to fill a vacancy in one of the Puerto Rican schools. You need to leave for Baltimore. It is a mission territory and it can be very hot there," announced the principal.

Again, the warning given by Father Mooney crossed Sister Mary's mind.

"You will be transferred to unknown places and maybe even to a foreign country if you join an international congregation."

Sister Mary was getting used to short notice travel. Calmness and acceptance began to increase with each new assignment.

Arriving at the motherhouse, she was met by Sister Othilda, a long time resident of Puerto Rico. She had arrived the week before after serving as director of novices of native Puerto Rican sisters.

"Sister Mary, you will not be going to Puerto Rico but leaving for our mission in Florida. Most of the students there are from families of Cuban immigrants. Sister Marie will be joining us. She just took final vows and has visitors today. We will be leaving early in the morning. Mass will be at eight o'clock, have a good breakfast and meet me at the front door at ten," directed the sister.

Holding her black suitcase, Sister Mary arrived at the front door. A smiling pretty sister was waiting, too. It was Sister Marie, the traveling companion.

"I am going to Florida. Where are you going?" asked the newly vowed sister.

"I am going to Florida also. You, too, must be traveling with Sister Othilda," offered Sister Mary.

Both religious were happy to be traveling together. They had time to get acquainted before it was time to leave. Sister Marie and Sister Mary were going to teach at different schools.

Both girls and even the novice director enjoyed the long train ride. It was an air-condition car and Sister Othilda brought along a good sized basket with sandwiches, fruit, cookies and she ordered soft drinks for the trip. The older sister entertained the two young women with stories of her early experiences when she first went to Puerto Rico.

"I didn't know the language, was assigned to a very poor mission. Most of the materials were in short supply and children had to share. It's different now. Our schools here in the United States send us supplies. They are very generous.

It is much more updated now. We have high schools there and even a college. I'll miss my adopted country," sister said.

The new arrivals were also given some admonitions on how to strive for holiness.

"A new member either brings blessings to a place or causes unrest and unhappiness. Spread the love of God and strengthen your prayer life."

On arrival at the Tampa train station, Sister Mary followed the sisters and when she descended from the train a wave of heat surrounded her. The temperature was high in Tampa and a recent rainfall generated a haze of hot steam.

Sisters were waiting for the new arrivals and they were immediately driven to their convents.

Sister Othilda and Sister Mary were driven to the front door of a two story buff brick building surrounded by stately palm trees. A lovely lawn fronted the convent and bushes bordered the entrance. In a few months the bushes would be covered with beautiful white carnations. Although there were houses in the area and a large school building was next to a high steepled church across the street. It seemed so quiet as the two sisters walked up to the closed door. Sister Phyllis, the superior, quickly answered the doorbell.

"We have been expecting you. Welcome! We are just completing our prayers and the sisters will be out soon. I'll show you to your rooms. When you have freshened up come into the community room. Sister Mary, there are three sisters from your profession class who are stationed here and Sister Cora will be your partner. We have two of every class, picking up a piece of luggage, the superior led the sisters to the upstairs sleeping area.

"What a nice room," thought Mary.

Her room was large, included a desk and glancing out of the large picture window, Mary had a beautiful view of a grassy open field. Twenty-four sisters made up the group of teachers that worked in the grade and high school. Some of the older sisters that had taught in Puerto Rico immediately bombarded Sister Othilda with questions.

Sister Rosa asked,

"Who is in charge of the novices now?"

"Sister Gracia, will be good and is taking over the program. She is a native, knows the language well and I am confident she will do very well."

Sister Mary was taken aside by the sisters that were with her as postulants and novices. They had become good friends during their training years. They exchanged bits of news and spent time recalling the past. Within a few days Sister Mary got right into the rhythm of the new convent routine. School would begin soon and immediately she and Sister Cora began planning for classes and getting classrooms ready for the start of the new school year. During one of the preparation days, puzzled, Sister Mary asked her school partner,

"I thought I was going to be stationed at one of the mission schools for the poor. The convent is such a modern and comfortable building. I don't understand."

"When the three of us came from the novitiate, we had a run down hut to live in. Termites had eaten almost all the wood. It was risky to open windows. Wood crumbled right in your hand. Beds were never made up until we were ready to retire. Termites had to be pulled out of the bedding. This is a recently built convent. It was ordered by the board of examiners. You came at a good time," explained Sister Cora.

Start of school went well and the new teacher quickly became attached to the students. Not only were they studious but always willing and enthusiastic for any additional project suggested. They enjoyed drama and were anxious to please. Class sizes were usually in the fifties. Large classes posed no problem. Parents insisted their children pay attention to the teacher and encouraged them to take advantage of the education of the newly adopted country.

Most of the children were first generation Cuban immigrants. Education was a high priority with the students as well as the parents. They believed in their lofty dreams and miracles. Their dreams came true. Many graduates of Our Lady's School became worthy citizens and well paid competent workers. The professionals were always grateful for the role of educators in their lives. Many kept in touch with their former teachers.

Students never flaunted their poverty. Fathers worked in the tobacco fields with meager wages and only had seasonal work. Fathers minded the idle times that unemployment created. The Cubans were proud men, good workers, devoted to family and committed employees.

The depth of their poverty was evident one cold, damp February morning. One of the girls arrived in the classroom very early. She shivered as she walked into the room. The teacher greeted the child. Clutching her coat, the girl confided,

"My house is so cold. I had to break up the ice on top of my basin of water before I could wash up this morning."

"Don't you have heat when it is cold and damp?" questioned sister.

"No, we put newspapers between blankets. That makes our beds warm," added the girl.

Sister Cora's discussion on the school children's needs came to mind. Several large wooden crates arrived in the school and were lined up against the stage of the auditorium.

"What are those huge boxes doing in this room?" enquired Sister Mary.

"They contain items to be sold at our big festival. We have one each spring. It helps pay for school supplies. My aunt sends them. They contain pre-inventory items. Those articles remain on the shelves too long and don't sell. We can price them low enough for quick sale. All the money we make is used for school supplies. Our students can't afford school supplies and books. Insufficient wages earned by fathers are needed for food and lodging.

When the festival days arrived, Sister Mary and her students were highly enthusiastic. The class was going to have a duck pond booth. It was all set up with a child's swimming pool centered in the allotted class space. Prizes were lined against the wall. Several toy ducks were floating in the pool. Droves of people filled the auditorium. This was her first experience at the fair and Sister Mary was anxious for a successful outcome.

On the second day of the fair, she expected her brother Francis and his wife Irene. They spent several weeks in

Florida each year. The couple had timed their stay in Florida to coincide with the festival. The morning of the second day was a disaster! The swimming pool sprung a leak. Members of the senior class, organizers of the affair, came to the rescue. Several young men cleaned up the mess with mops and buckets very much in sight. A forlorn group stood on the sideline!

When Francis appeared and asked for Sister Mary, two of the seniors led the couple to the teacher with her group of sad looking students.

"Where is your booth?" asked Francis.

The students, all speaking at one time, excitedly and with disappointing tones, told the couple of the tragic demise of the pool and their enterprise.

"Irene and I will fix that," Francis said. Set up your counter and in about an hour we will be in business again."

What seemed forever but was only a two hour wait, Francis and Irene returned with a dart sets. The upper classmen came to the rescue again and in a short time, happy students and a smiling teacher were ready to meet the large crowd that came to see what the lively commotion was all about. They did very well the remaining days.

Francis and Irene enjoyed their visits to Our Lady's Convent. They were always impressed with the joyful spirit, and friendliness of the religious. Other members of the Tantalo family that visited Florida included Patricia, Joseph and Lucy. Not all of the sisters had visitors. Travel was expensive and Tampa was too far away.

Final vow time was fast approaching. Four of the sisters at Our Lady's Convent in Florida would be taking vows the following summer. Directives were mailed from the motherhouse. The sisters were given assigned readings. Preparation requirements were a time of discernment, reflection, self-examination and prayer. There would be a lengthy retreat before the trial time expired. Each of the four sisters at Our Lady's Convent must decide if she could live a vowed life. Sister Mary recalled the Canonical examination that preceded her novitiate.

"What makes you want to be a religious? Are you being influenced by anyone?" the clergyman had asked many like questions.

"I suppose we will have the same questions asked and of course, there will be reports and letters from our former superiors," thought Sister Mary.

Three religious from Sister Mary's profession class did not take final vows. The four sisters returning from Baltimore had a joyous return ride to Florida. Often, newly vowed sisters received assignment transfers the year they took vows.

A few years after final vows, Sister Mary became ill and needed surgery. Although the operation was a success the sister was not getting her strength back. Tampa's damp heat triggered off a respiratory problem. The head nurse at the motherhouse recommended she return to the North Country.

The long stay at Our Lady's School and Convent made the thought of transfer intolerable. Sister Mary was attached to the students.

"I'll miss these sisters. They are a great bunch of women and a prayerful group who are always ready to help and fun to be with," thought the religious.

Her next assignment took her to Connecticut. A new structure was being built on the parish property. It was a new School to accommodate the young families that were building homes in Fairfield County. Classrooms were added each year. Sister Ellen taught the fifth grade class but was being transferred. A sudden illness made the transfer necessary for Sister Ellen. Sister Mary was to fill the vacancy at St. Theresa's School.

Here again she was greeted with such warmth and kindness that she immediately became part of a very happy young community. Both the school and Convent were situated in a rural area and reminded the Florida newcomer of her home in Rochester.

Students at St. Theresa's, however, were very different from her classes in Tampa. They were self-composed, intelligent and scholarly. Many of the young parents were professionals that made demands on their children. Although the children in Tampa were good students, they weren't competitive with the determination and vigor that was new to Sister Mary. They were more like her sisters Patricia, Amy and brother Joseph.

The experienced teacher began to use individualized methods.

"These students like mind challenges. I'll give them that," the teacher resolved.

It was amazing and gratifying at the positive responses from so many of the young people. Each student was allowed to go at his/her own pace. Groups of students with like interests   worked together while individual pupils explored on their own.

Preparation time for classes could be exhausting but Sister Mary was able to cope very well despite the large class with almost sixty students. Students at Saint Theresa's were self-motivated. The Sister, however, was not completely free of stress. Studies were on going in the life of a School Sister of Notre Dame. Since Sister Mary had an aptitude for numbers she was working towards her masters in math. She signed up for rigorous courses that were being taught by a Jesuit priest. The drop out rate of his classes was high. The course was too expensive to drop out of or quit. There were times that she was still struggling with a problem as late as midnight. Classes were held three evenings a week.

Added tasks were often assigned to the experienced teachers. Most of the sisters at St. Theresa's taught late afternoon religion classes to students in neighboring parishes that did not have their own schools. A Catholic college in the region also frequently invited qualified sisters to teach method's courses to students working on education degrees. Leisure was quite rare due to the multi task filled day.

When Pope John twenty-third became pope, many changes were taking place in the church as well as convents. School Sisters of Notre Dame were changing into a more modified habit. The new habit had less material and the head covering was not so bulky. Other changes in the habit soon followed. Sisters were given permission to drive and, therefore, could wear professional secular clothing such as suits. Safe driving necessitated freedom to see and hear well. Non-veil driving was encouraged to give sisters greater visibility and keener hearing while driving.

Another great and welcome change was that of enclosure. The School Sisters of Notre Dame were no longer a semi-cloistered congregation. Their active ministry, that of educators, made demands that made enclosure impractical. Radical societal changes were taking place. It was imperative that the teaching sisters were skilled communicators. Added skills were needed to promote the health of body, mind and spirit of the modern child.

Additionally, enclosure changes revised home visit rules. Visits to family members were being made. Sister Mary made her first home visit soon after the enclosure changes. Notre Dame Sisters, moreover, began attending classes in secular colleges and universities. Shopping was no longer delegated to members of the parish. The sisters were able to go to stores to make their own purchases.

At the completion of ten years at St. Theresa's, Sister Mary was transferred to a Rochester school where she taught math and science to eighth graders for three years. A new technology age was emerging. Digital approach to numbers was also taking place. One of the corporations in Rochester was introducing computers in the late sixties. Sister Mary attended classes being offered. When the principal questioned on the usefulness of the studies, Sister Mary responded,

"Computers are an expensive item. I suppose prices will be in the thousands. It will be a while before we can afford them."

"In that case, better not continue the courses. You are already working for your masters in library media," suggested the principal.

As she was completing the third year at the Rochester school, she received a call from a provincial councilor. They needed a superior and principal in a rural school.

"I am not comfortable with being a superior and I do not have a degree in administration," was Sister Mary's response.

"Well, we can do without a superior. Convents are starting shared responsibility. You will be assigned as principal and begin studies for certification in administration. You expressed the desire to work as school media specialist. You will be better at the post once you have served your term as principal," suggested the provincial leader.

The new assignment as administrator had many challenging aspects that fascinated Sister Mary. The new school was in the New York diocese. It was a recently built small school erected in the dairy farm area. Students came from low to medium income families. Fathers of students were New York City policemen and firemen. Some were dairy farmers or worked as black dirt onion growers.

An animal lover, the new principal of St. Edward's was delighted with the beautiful country school. There were many signs of farm life during the school day. The second day of school, amazingly, cows from the neighboring dairy farm, crossed the road and roamed about the schoolyard. Undisturbed by children calling out the windows, the cows peacefully, and leisurely kept right on nibbling the grassy area around the building. A smiling teacher appeared in the principal's office,

"Just phone Mrs. Penny, she will come over and shoo them back to their territory."

Near the end of the first year as principal, 1973, a phone call was received from the provincial leader,

"This is your silver jubilee year. You are scheduled to spend the summer at the motherhouse in Rome for renewal. Are your travel plans in place?" questioned the Provincial.

"I was not planning to go," said the sister principal.

"This is a spiritual renewal program. You have been keeping up with studies. That is a good thing. However, don't you think it is even more important to renewal spiritually? If the convent does not have funds, the motherhouse will provide you with travel expenses," recommended the leader.

Of course, Sister Mary made the trip and did spend the summer with sisters that had been professed in 1948. Sisters participating in the renewal class included long time friends that were trained together in Baltimore. Since the School Sisters of Notre Dame are an international congregation, many sisters from other countries were also present. Amazingly, they were able to communicate with each other. The first weekend in Rome was a free one. Sisters had the option to visit nearby towns and cities. Sister Mary made the decision to visit relatives east of Rome, birthplace of her parents.

It was a quaint village, LaVilla, bordering one of the national parks. Her greatest delight was examining ancestral sites. It was a mountainous region, with small farms, sheep grazing and folks that attended daily Mass at the church in the center of the small village. Surprisingly, her cousins spoke English. She was given a tour of family sites, an abundance of heritage information and the greatest treat of all, visited the school where her grandmother taught. Most female family members were either teaching or into educational studies.

When Sister Mary returned to Rome, she was loaded with exposed film of village pictures and an large amount of valuable information. It was an added unexpected treat that was shared with family members many times. It also awakened a desire for the unencumbered   spirituality of her ancestors.

Within a few days of the renewal program in Rome, Sister Mary was seized with a strong desire for true holiness. Renewal days brought back the joys of the contemplative period spent during the canonical year as novice. Again, there was another searching into heritage, the legacy of the church and the founders of the congregation.

Spiritual leaders of the Church and congregation shared theological insights, and prayed with the sisters on their extended retreat. Visits were made to shrines, the catacombs and centers with wealthy writings of some of the great saints of the Church. Sister Mary and her friends felt enriched, rested and were very grateful as they returned to the United States.

On her return to St. Edward's School at the end of the trip to Rome, Sister Mary quickly became reacquainted with the fast paced days of a principal. Days, months and even years sped by swiftly. It had been a well functioning school even before Sister Mary took over the principalship of St. Edward's. Little changes were needed to keep it running smoothly with dedicated faculty and children ready to learn.

The administrator of a small school with happy cooperative parents and fine teachers, made the new job rewarding. There was a longing, however, for teaching. When the term of administrator came to an end, the principal requested a teaching assignment.

14
Great Changes

Family members were delighted when Mary was assigned to the co-institutional school in Rochester. BK High was a large suburban school. Students shared many of the major facilities such as cafeteria, gym and library. Boys' classes as well as girls', however, were in separate buildings of the same complex. Nonetheless, some classes were co-ed such as AP courses, music, art and library research.

The principal of the school had asked for a librarian. It was a Middle States Certified school, therefore, needed enough media specialists to satisfy total population needs of both schools. After meeting with the principal before classes began, Sister Mary was asked to include an additional teaching task to her schedule.

"I've spoken with the librarian and although there is great need of an assistant, she agreed to limit your time. There is a shortage of teachers in the math and skills departments. Can you take these classes for this first year?"

"Math is a major interest of mine and certainly, no problem taking classes. I've already met with Sister Marie.

She acquainted me with the present need of more teachers and is willing to modify the schedule," replied Sister Mary.

School Sisters of Notre Dame taught the girls' classes and the Christian Brothers taught the young men.

Catholic Schools had begun employing lay teachers. If a vacancy occurred and no religious was available, young men and women living in the area applied. Most of the young lay teachers working at BK were graduates of the school and, therefore, were familiar with the school's philosophy and mission. Sister Mary always found these young men and women great colleagues. It was remarkable that these talented teachers were willing to work for meager salaries. The Church realized the injustice of these wages and is now paying faculty members salaries commensurate with colleagues in the public schools. To keep tuition affordable for the average family income, salaries were one way of keeping full building enrollment in the Catholic schools. During the late sixties, some religious teachers were receiving as little as thirty dollars a month. Lay teachers, however, were never paid such low wages.

In the 1970s, over 75% of the BK faculty was made up of young Irish Christian Brothers and School Sisters of Notre Dame. They were a lively and happy group. It was a contagious joy that spilled over to the whole school. Families were very much part of the school. The school's band was in constant demand. Demands for their performances took them not only out of state but also to foreign lands. Family members as well as faculty members accompanied the students traveling to foreign countries.

Other school activities, clubs, sports, plays, dances and parent group activities kept teacher moderators in the building evenings. A number of teachers at BK had charge of more than one activity. Sister Mary guided the Future Teachers' Club her first year. When she became library director, she worked with the library and Audio Visual clubs. New students immediately became involved in activities and/or sports.

Gone was the quiet and leisure for long periods of private prayer and contemplation of Rome and the Novitiate. The spirit of prayer is a continuous process with religious.

Students and teachers were often found in the school's chapels during their free time. Student planned liturgies were frequently taking place in these chapels.

The first great challenge Sister Mary confronted at BK was to improve non-regents students study habits and to stimulate a love of learning. Only strong desires, confidence and success could bring on self-motivation. Lighting the spark for a love of learning was the key.

Pupils were introduced to materials and topics of interest that included several levels of ability. Unless a student met with a fair amount of success, frustration and paralysis set in. Only a courageous approach to studies was needed to thaw off fear of failure and dissatisfaction.

Although both the girls' and boys' classes were large, Sister Mary initiated an individualized program. The method would allow each student to start at a comfortable level and taken to the highest point the learner aimed for. Seniors from the video club were called on to tape the classes in action. Reviewing their performances via TV shots did much to bolster the young peoples' image of success.

Video men were clever, using impromptu interviews to bolster a student's self esteem.

"Dan, you are searching several sources. You seem to be having great success, what is your topic?" the cameraman might ask.

Such questions were often interjected and the seniors had great success with students. Within a few weeks, the club members were doing a great job motivating the young men and women. These media men were a blessing. It was an almost miraculous transfer of video men taking over a great part of the instruction. The aim of the skills courses was to raise students' academic level. Most of the students were transferred to regent's classes after completing the individualized skills program.

Technology was fast advancing use of PCs in education. Hardware was expensive and therefore schools hesitated to adopt courses that used personal computers. Chief administrator of BK, Brother Brian, was a science major with interest in current advances in the field.

An intelligent and fine computer technician was hired to teach computer science. A few members of the library and video clubs were taking Mr. Miller's computer classes. They were excited and motivated Sister Mary to quickly look into computer use. With limited budget, she decided to approach the budding interest with caution. The media teacher questioned Mr. Miller on the future of the computer and its role in the library. He immediately assured her that computers would be a must in education and a great tool of library research. In fact Mr. Miller offered Sister Mary his old computer to use in the library and suggested she get acquainted with the new equipment.

The PC was an old TRs 80 with limited memory of 4K. Video club members were excited that there was a computer to use in the library. There was a contest going on.

The computer teacher was offering a cash prize for any program written up by a student. The software had to be practical and useful. Computer students asked for suggestions on a needed topic. Sister Mary suggested several topics and one of the students, Pat Smith, picked on a winning topic. He wrote up a useful item to use for book acquisitions. It won the prize. Pat received news publicity that motivated not only students but faculty members as well.

Rochester was in a fine library system. Parochial schools were often invited to participate in secular subject exchanges. One of the most productive exchanges took place between the public and private school librarians. A great leader of the exchanges included Sharon Johnson. She met with high school library media specialist several times a year. Computer workshops were offered to all. Technology played a great role in topic exchanges.

Confidence in the use of computers took hold and PCs were being included in libraries.

Teaching and introducing students to multiple research tools that included the new technologies were not the only source of contentment for Sister Mary. There was camaraderie among members of the faculty that made for many happy days. The cheerful relaxed climate of BK gave students courage to seek out teachers if they were troubled.

Family problems were beginning to seep into a pupil's school day. Startled at the sudden drop in test scores of a student, the teacher approached his guidance counselor.

"You are asking me if there is a reason for John's drop in marks? That is understandable. He has an unbelievable home problem. Last week his sleep was disturbed by a loud thumping sound on the side porch. His parents are separated and John is the eldest of four children. On hearing the sound, frightened, he picked up his baseball club and went to investigate. He called out to his mother and other members of the family that an intruder   was trying to get into the house. The mother in nightclothes, ran up to her son screaming and pleading not to strike the man. She admitted to the four children that although the man was a stranger to them, he was her boyfriend.

This is a bad time for John. We are getting help for the family. If you recall, a few days last week, he was not in school. We were meeting with his father. There are many problems that need attention. Please be very kind to the boy," Brother McFarland informed the teacher.

Sister Mary was saddened by the news. This was an incident that occurred in the late 1970s. It was an uncommon incident in her experiences.

Humor and good fun was often part of the school day. Students were relatively happy young men and women. Always ready to divert from the day's lesson, harmless pranks frequently surfaced. On one occasion, Sister Mary was a few minutes late for one of the classes. Habitually prompt, Sister frowned on latecomers. Her students learned that promptness was important to their teacher. When she walked into the room a few minutes late, students arranged their desks to face the rear of the room instead of facing the teacher. Baffled, Sister Mary decided to give them a like treatment. She, too, turned her desk and faced the front wall. Silence prevailed for several minutes. Finally two students walked up to the sister's desk and turned it around as the pupils, too, moved to face the front of the room. Laughter broke the silence.

Tuition cost rose yearly and parents made sacrifices to send children to Catholic schools. When students were old enough to find jobs, they learned to balance home assignments with job schedules. Sister Mary often rewarded a good class performance by giving the last ten minutes of the period to begin home assignments.

Relaxing strict enclosure rules gave nuns time for home visits. Unlike the early nineteen hundreds family members were moving away from family centered neighborhoods. Small farms and large country land tracts were being developed into heavy populated suburbs. After World War Two, young married couples frequently moved to distant cities. Travel was becoming popular and air travel was more common.

Two of Sister Mary's brothers had moved to California, Francis still remained in Malone. Her brother Fred and all her sisters had moved to the suburbs. Although visiting family members was allowed, the school's scheduled evening activities limited time spent with brothers and sisters. Visits were treasured. Rides to family homes always required advance planning. There were only two cars available to sisters living at the BK Convent. Cars were shared among the sisters once numbering as many as twenty-four.

Sister Mary was appalled at some of the devastating changes in Rochester when she returned after more than her thirty years absence. Arriving by plane, the cab ride to the convent exposed the passengers to a ravaged urban inner city.

"What ever happened to Bausch and Lomb, the optical factory? It's empty, and every window is broken. These buildings are in such disrepair," questioned the native of Rochester.

"Factories, too, are moving their plants to the suburbs to avoid graffiti and broken windows by unruly and destructive vandals," answered the cab driver.

Ravages brought on by poverty became more evident each year. Family owned factories and department stores that had been founded by hard working Rochester natives were making great corporate changes. These visible transformations were taking place in the nineteen eighties.

Employees no longer saw employers. Gone were the days when an employer would mingle among the workers.

Mergers were taking place, out of town searches for influential corporate high salaried leaders were being made. These high-ranking chiefs were included in all decision-making. Mergers often meant that title changes, along with alterations in policies meant lay-offs, reduced benefits and even moving plants to other states and countries.

Heads of families were no longer confident that they would be kept on the job till retirement. If a trained worker was fired, employment in the same skill would not be available. After unemployment checks ceased, lower paid jobs had to be taken. Wives no longer were stay at home mothers. Both parents needed employment to raise a family.

Couples that were capable parents could not afford having large families.

This was the situation that students' parents were facing during the last decade of the twentieth century.

Religious congregations were not admitting young applicants until they were secure in their career choices. Therefore, lay teachers were replacing religious in Catholic schools. Tuition hikes were needed to pay these dedicated qualified teachers. Many students found jobs as soon as they were of age. Realizing the struggle their parents were under, these young men and women helped pay for their tuition. More often, a Catholic education was not affordable.

Teachers at BK made every effort to keep budgets at a bare bones level. In the mid nineteen eighties a tuition hike was being considered. When the library clerk retired, Sister Mary chose to get along without the clerk. Clerical needs of the library were met by volunteers and added evening hours for the media specialist.

Accredited schools were often asked to submit names of staff members. Selected members served on teams that spent several days visiting a school. Sister Mary served on such teams. One afternoon, after completing assessment tasks of an academy in Buffalo, Sister Mary phoned the convent. She would be returning to Rochester that same day. Sister Grace's response seemed strange. There was almost complete silence on the other end of the line.

"Is something wrong?" enquired Sister Mary.

"Yes, we just returned from Paul Blake's funeral," was the solemn reply.

The religious was speechless at the reply. Paul was the president of the video club. The fine young man had spoken to Sister Mary on the morning she was leaving for Buffalo. They were discussing last minute details of materials deliveries to classrooms.

"Sister, don't worry about a thing. The video club men will make sure that all deliveries are made on time. Now, don't you worry, all is going to be fine," the young man assured the teacher.

"What a special fellow, that Paul. He is almost too good to be true," thought Sister Mary as she left the library for her out of town evaluation assignment.

Although still in shock at the message, Sister Mary asked, "What happened?"

"Paul was driving his young brother and sisters the evening you left Rochester. It was Halloween evening and the big brother took them around for tricks and treat. He returned the children home safely but on his way to pick up the older girl, his car went out of control. It hit a light pole and he was killed almost instantly. It was a rainy windy night with leaves and wet pavement making roads slippery," Sister Grace told the saddened religious.

When Sister Mary returned to the convent late afternoon, she immediately went to Chapel. Several sisters were already there. All were aware of the effect the accident would have on the sister. Their strong sympathetic support was very evident. Sister Annie, the prayerful eldest sister, instantly came up to the distressed teacher,

"The candle to the far right of the altar has been burning for Paul and his family since the tragedy," the nun offered.

On her return to school the next day, Sister Mary felt the full impact of the heartbreaking accident. Members of the Video and Library Clubs spoke of the tragedy with tears and whispers. Many members of Paul's classes as well as the club members came up to the teacher. Sometimes the students came in groups but at other times they came singly. All attested to what a great guy Paul was. They spoke of the wake, and especially the funeral. What surprised and what was reassuring was the attitude displayed by Paul's classmates. Students spoke of their friends goodness, his love of family and great faith.

"Sister, I am sure Paul is with God now. He must be happy and we can pray to him as our saint."

"Paul was such a good person. At the funeral Mass, we all agreed that we were gifted to have known him. He is in heaven. I'll sure miss him," were a few of comments made.

Speaking to family members, shortly after the accident, the teacher shared some of her feelings and comments of the young people. Paul's parents, people of deep faith, were not only accepting but also grateful for the gift of their son.

"We will miss our Paul so very much but what a treasure his sixteen years of life were to all of us. There will forever be an empty place in our hearts for the dear one but what a beautiful memory we have," the mother tearfully shared.

As the years passed, Sister Mary found time to visit family some week ends, holidays and vacation time. Visits included trips to Francis home in Malone but most of the visits were to members of her family living in Rochester.

This afforded many happy days filled with cheerful chatter, teasing and sumptuous Italian meals. Very often family gatherings were at the home of Patricia's and Lucy's large Greek revival home in Churchville.

Churchville was a small village between Rochester and Buffalo. The original family gathering home near Highland Park had been among the homes needed by the state to widen the highway. The home on Highland Avenue had been demolished but the land lay barren. Patricia and Lucy purchased the Churchville home after much searching and thought.

Their brother did not approve of the purchase. Aside from the large size of the house, he objected to the rural area it was located on.

"Why do you want to live in a sparsely populated village with no near neighbors? You are both doing very well now with homes in the safe suburbs. I am afraid of your safety," he argued.

"We both have dogs. They are friendly with family members or friends and both are great protectors," was the usual response.

It was a large white house on a four acre rural area. The front lawn was lush with huge chestnut trees and tall blue spruce pines. A big picturesque interesting barn was behind the house. There was a quaint Quonset hut on the side. Fruit trees fronted a vegetable garden. Previous owners were proud to give the historical background of the estate and assured the two new owners that the fertile soil had never been tainted with insecticides.

The young women had been hesitant and delayed the purchase. It was much too immense. Ten rooms plus a large space for expansion would be a challenge. The untainted soil of the property was immediately attractive. Overly used food insecticides had begun to be a big concern of many.

While the two women decided to purchase the house, both were having job challenges. Patricia was credit manager of her company. In her work as Para legal, Lucy was in the midst of a career change. An educator searching for workers noticed her interview skills with young men and women. Wayward habitual unskilled young lawbreakers needed training. Lucy lost no time getting certified and held the teaching job until she was again impelled to be caregiver of the youngest family member, Amy.

When the BK teacher took time to visit at the Churchville home, she returned to school rested, energized and renewed. One of the upstairs sections that included a small sitting room adjacent to a bedroom was set up for Sister Mary's exclusive use. Patricia and Lucy fitted this secluded part of the house where the religious could spend time for prayer, reading, study or lesson preparations.

There was always a driver available to take the teacher to the country home in Churchville. The Notre Dame Sisters came in twos or threes. They would stay for refreshments, chatter and often remained for a meal before returning to the Convent. They, too, liked the set up. On first examining Mary's quarters, remarks followed the first exposure,

"I like the view from this window. Sit on the rocker and use it as a reading or prayer place." Some other remarks that followed,

"I like the mahogany desk and view from the side. It faces the large orchard."

"Sister Mary, this is a fine retreat place. You only need to visit your sisters Pat and Lucy to make your yearly retreat."

In casual attire and dressed for the weather, be it warm or cold, Mary enjoyed the long walks about the wooded area, while meditating, reading from the breviary or just getting pleasure by watching the little animals moving about. There were playful little creatures such as chipmunks, squirrels, and raccoons always scurrying about the grounds.

Many tranquil periods of quiet prayer were spent at the country place. The religious tried to recapture the contemplative mode that prevailed during her time of renewal in Rome or the Novitiate.

"How nice to have such a nice place to visit. Thank you, God for such a caring family. I really came to the convent to thank God for all the blessings bestowed on my family. Here I am enjoying it all again," thought Mary.

One quiet Saturday afternoon, while walking about the grounds, a car drove up with two young women. At first the nun did not recognize them. When they walked up to Sister Mary, to her surprise, Antoinette Parr and Pat Costa were the visitors.

"It can't be true. What are you doing in Rochester?" asked the nun.

"We are here to visit our family and thought we would surprise you. Your sisters said that you are now working in Rochester," laughingly said Antoinette. Patricia and Lucy soon appeared on the scene. The visitors were expected and Lucy thought it would be a nice surprise for them to get together and get reacquainted. In the course of the conversation, Antoinette asked,

"I thought you were a semi cloistered congregation. You never wrote and were not allowed to visit unless for serious illness or death of parents. Are you still in the convent? You are not wearing a habit or veil."

"To your last question. I am still very much a nun. There have been many changes in our constitution. Much of the changes were due to the documents of the Second Vatican Council. Times are changing, and the needs of the world make it necessary to adjust to the times. We are an active international congregation, very much aware of the needs of the poor. After all, most congregations were founded in the nineteenth century to take care of the needs of immigrants here in the United States. Founders of religious orders opened schools, orphanages and hospitals for the poor. There are now other more pressing needs. Relaxing strict enclosure rules can make us aware of these needs by mingling and understanding the problems of the people we serve," her friend affirmed.

Frequently, long ago friends as well as relatives visited Sister Mary either at her sisters' home or at the Convent. The convent was on the top floor of the girls' school. When she first came to Rochester, in nineteen seventy-four, there were twenty-four religious living at the BK Convent. Many of the Sisters as well as teachers of the school became life long friends not only of the religious but also of family members. During her retirement years at the Notre Dame Motherhouse, Sister Mary often recalled the support, kindnesses and help she received from her Community and friends.

Early one January cold morning, Sister Mary was traumatized by a phone call. It was from her sister Lucy.

"Mary, I am at the hospital. Amy has been in emergency since early last evening. They are taking tests.

You know she has been feeling lethargic since her bout with the flu."

"I'll have one of the sisters drive me there. I'm sure the principal will find a teacher substitute for me," offered the religious.

"Why don't you wait until after classes? The doctors have scheduled tests for most of the day. We will have some answers then," suggested Lucy.

Recalling the comment that Sister Madonna once made and her answer, her foretelling now came to pass. She recalled the statement and answer.

"You are so fortunate to have such a large number of brothers and sisters. What happiness is yours," said Sister Madonna long ago.

"Yes, it is a great blessing, however, I dread the time when there will be sickness and death to cope with. Will I be able to handle so many sorrows?" Sister Mary had responded.

It was one of those heartbreaking days. Sister Mary shared the news with the sisters of her community. There were many offers to drive her to the hospital. It was Sister Justene who finally drove Sister Mary to visit Amy.

"I go by the hospital every afternoon to pick up my sister Tean from work. I'll be happy to drive you."

One of the other sisters suggested that when it was time to be picked up, give a phone call. No problem picking her up, the religious was assured.

Entering the hospital room, the religious was relieved. Instead of seeing two forlorn and tearful young women, Amy and Lucy were laughing and teasing the nurse and doctor.

"What ever is going on here, why aren't the two of you at work? Are you having a party?" laughingly teased the older sister.

After the hugs and greetings, Sister Mary was introduced to the medical staff present in the room. The doctor spoke openly and frankly.

"Your sister Amy is a pretty sick girl. She is having a serious reaction from the medication she has been prescribed and has been taking it for almost a year. Her body frame is much too small for the high dosages she has been taking. We can't be certain, but most likely, decalcification has taken place. She has several problems walking and sitting up," soberly answered the medical man. This was the first of many hospital stays.

There were several discussions about Amy's health after she returned home from the hospital. Of the many choices suggested, Amy felt selling her large home and moving to a small apartment would be wise. It was a comfortable and charming apartment not too far from Churchville. She was also thinking of taking medical leave.

The youngest family member managed very well for a few years. She worked part time and curtailed many of her social activities. Like most members of the family, Amy liked to entertain. She could no longer have large group dinner parties.

"We will have joint entertainments," suggested the Churchville women. "After all, you know Frances expects us to include her and her friends when there is a holiday. We like that and it would be fun to have you join us when you can," continued Lucy. There was ample room for overnight guests. Sister Mary, Frances and Amy often stayed several days. Many happy times followed this arrangement. It was also quite a learning experience for the religious.

An interesting episode took place early one morning at the Churchville house. While Sister Mary was vacationing there during the Christmas holidays, she would hear the phone ring at five-thirty each morning. Lucy did not have many vacation days during that week. The School District teacher left for work each morning about seven o'clock.

"What is that phone call that comes in each morning?" enquired the religious.

"That is one of Lucy's students. It is a signal that she is up and will not be late for school. It's an arrangement made at the request of her brother who is serving a lengthy jail term. He attributes all his troubles to absenting himself from school," Pat replied.

Educators began to need more than subject content matter and the ability to teach. Children returned to their empty homes at the end of the school day. Frequently, even the very young used a key to get into the house and had to fend for themselves until a parent returned from work. Many came from single parent homes. Home assignments were often neglected. Some students, after parents left for work, didn't get up to go to school but played truant. This habit of not getting to school became addictive. It was a habit difficult to break.

Teachers at BK High School were grateful for the caring cooperative parents of the students. Although they, too, were beginning to feel the impact of a slumping economy, numerous students recognized parents' needs and helped when they were able. These fortunate parents had children who were self disciplined. Some young men and women were able to say no when need be and several had truly sacrificial attitudes.

Occasionally School Sisters of Notre Dame gathered in certain areas. Members of all the convents in the district met with their provincial leaders to discuss needs of people they served and changes required to be more effective. They had always ministered to the poor, youth and woman. Due to societal changes and economy slumps, many additional demands had to be met. Religious were being encouraged to reflect on their apostolates and if need be, make requests for additional training.

These changes became apparent to Sister Mary one afternoon. She was in the convent kitchen when she noticed Sister Justine filling foil trays with food. Curiously, she asked,

"What are you doing?"

"These are meals I am preparing for my nieces and nephew. Their mother abandoned them and my brother has problems cooking for them when he returns from work. These are leftovers from yesterday. My sister-in-law is having problems coping with her four young children and left home. When I shared their predicament with the sisters, they encouraged me to help out by going to their home with ready cooked meals."

"I'm sorry but I think it's great that we can now help our own, too," the religious asserted.

Members of the convent at BK were enthusiastic teachers and were always ready to join in evening school activities. Plays, dances and sports events were well attended by both the Notre Dame Sisters and the Christian Brothers.

Basketball games were Sister Mary's favorite. She tended to scream too loud when she got carried away with a successful throw. When the religious was not at a game, monitoring a dance or other activity, Sister Mary would be working in the library. It was not unusual to remain until ten o'clock. She often paused and reflected on her life of prayer. Although she never missed morning Mass, morning and afternoon prayer sessions, her night private prayer sessions were full of distractions. It was a constant battle to keep task and student needs out of her thoughts. She valued her yearly retreat week or quiet time in Churchville to get better prayer focus. These chore-oriented days would shortly change. Anxiety and concern would soon take up most of her thoughts.

It was another wintry dark snowy day when the religious received a phone call from her sister Lucy.

"Amy was rushed to the hospital I just arrived and will be here all day. Pat will be picking me up before dark. Can you stop up before I leave for Churchville?" asked the sister.

"Of course. It is two o'clock. I'll leave with Sister Justene. She will drive me I'm sure. I should be there about four-thirty. Is that OK?" anxiously questioned Mary. A new routine began for the religious. She was grateful that a sister was not only willing to drive her to the hospital every afternoon but she did it winningly and with concern.

Recurrently, when Lucy arrived at the hospital shortly after breakfast trays had been given out, she noticed that trays were left out of reach of the patient.

"Nothing would make me lose my appetite faster than if food was near and out of reach for a long period of time. That's why I try to be here for meals," Lucy confided to Sister Mary.

The conversation took place in the hospital lounge as Pat and Lucy were leaving. It was after dark, a time that Patricia didn't like to drive. She never liked driving the country roads late nights. Pat would never complain and would cope with the situation. Amy's dogs, as well as their two dogs were left at the house. Mornings, after Patricia left Lucy off, she went to work, returned to feed the animals, prepare supper and then return to the hospital to pick up Lucy. The religious had a solution. No need for Pat to have all that extra fear of driving nights.

"It is very convenient for Sister Justene to drop me off here at four in the afternoon. It's no problem for me to have supper here at the hospital. Pat, pick Lucy up earlier and I can be here for her evening meal," offered the religious.

Amy was a joy to be with. She was so young to be infirm. Although in her forties, she still had that girlish appearance. Light haired, with large brown eyes and such a beautiful contagious smile. She seldom complained, spoke little of her sickness but she was quick to tell members of the family what the doctors' reports were. This hospital stay lasted almost three weeks.

Weekend visits to Churchville resumed soon after Amy's hospital discharge. One of the Friday evenings, soon after she returned from work, Amy was upset and confided in her sisters.

"Jerry, one of the law partners, suggested I quit work if I am going to take so much time off. My boss urged me to let it pass. He said Jerry didn't have much to say on personnel decisions and the other two lawyers needed me and had no problem with the time off."

Lucy responded quickly.

"Quit! I've been thinking, why don't you take time off? Let's open an antique business. Pat, tell Amy. We have so many items that should be sold. Carl, the antique dealer, suggested that to me so often. You've seen the Quonset hut.

There just isn't any more room in there. All we need to do is open the doors and advertise," animatedly encouraged Lucy.

"Good idea," Pat encouraged. "There is so much stuff in the hut, I have nightmares thinking about it. It will take a life time to get rid of it," laughingly added Patricia.

"I know Carl. Isn't he the fellow that was walking toward the hut one morning last summer? He looked so suspicious, that I told Pat and ran to the hut, fearing he was up to no good. Lucy, you just smiled and he was showing you a comb he had just purchased. He wanted you to price it for him. He comes over once in a while and likes animals. Is that the Carl you mean?" Asked Sister Mary.

"That's the guy. Mary, you looked so comical that day. You were really frightened," was Lucy's response.

The laughter that followed eased the tension and Amy, too joined in the fun.

"What about your teaching job. You like it," added Amy.

"I like to teach. I can tutor. I do that now anyway. I hate driving all that way to school each morning. The icy roads are so treacherous winters, I'd rather sell antiques. Besides, Amy, remember how we used to go to pawn shops on Front Street to buy interesting junk when we were young? The boys were always going to snitch to Papa but they never did. As we sell, we can also purchase. It will be fun going to antique shows and country roads in search of items." With the comment, it became a done deal.

Within a few months, and at the start of the school year, business cards were printed, the quonset doors were opened with the two women very much into antiques and collectibles. Vegetables had been planted in the fertile soil. Many of them were ripe, freshly picked lettuce had already been eaten and still growing. Health food stores in the area were constantly ready to purchase from organic farms. Lucy had been studying farm literature giving instructions on how to substitute non-poisonous materials to kill insects, halt diseases and the use of safe fertilizers.

Frequently, after a brief visit to Churchville, Sister Mary would be given fresh produce for the convent.

"You should be selling it instead of giving it away," the sister driver would comment.

"Better that friends and family eat vegetables and fruit from this untainted soil," Lucy would reply.

The young people of the library and video clubs were often invited to the country home. It was an ideal place for them to hold their yearly picnic exploring the barn, playing with the dogs and have a day away from school. Students of courses in architecture were among the club members. They would examine the structure of the Greek revival house and study like buildings in the little village.

Meetings, services given, and relationships enriched club members with like interest with students from other classes. Memberships were valued and life long friendships would develop. They were great support groups for those in need. Unfortunately, rejections could be devastating for a young person. An event that left Sister Mary feeling hopelessly inadequate and angry occurred the day after a club picnic.

"Greta, a club member, came into the library office as the homeroom bell was ringing.

"Sister, I need a small place where I can be alone," sobbingly asked the young student.

"Sure, lets try the magazine room. It will be free for the next two periods," suggested the teacher.

It was a room off the library that held back issues of magazines, newspapers and valuable documents. After the sister made sure the student was comfortable and satisfied, she closed the door behind her. No need to question the young woman. She was too distraught. The religious informed the office that Greta would be in the library for a confidential meeting. Let her teachers know that she was in the building and would meet her instructors after school to pick up the work she had missed.

The girl was given almost a half-hour to compose herself. When the teacher came into the room, Greta was wiping her eyes and at the same time looking at a magazine.

"Here is a glass of water and also a coke, you have a choice. I don't often give choices you know. Take advantage and be my guest," teased the puzzled teacher. "Do you want me to call your guidance counselor or would you like to call home? What can I do for you?" Asked the teacher.

"Sister, I have a real problem that I will have the rest of my life. Jack invited me to the junior prom yesterday while I was at the picnic. Of course, I said yes. He met me at my locker this morning and said he can't take me. His mother objected. She said I am a nigger with a black father." With that, the sobs returned.

"You don't have a problem. It's Jack and his mother that have a big, big problem. First of all, be glad that you are not going with him. You are such an intelligent, pretty girl with a great personality. You can have your pick of escorts. I am more concerned about Jack. He has a lot to learn and will have a very unhappy life if he doesn't do something before it is too late. Do you mind if I say something to the priest chaplain? Would you like to talk to Father David? How can I help?" The sister continued.

"Sister, I feel better already. I'll just go to classes and pretend that I don't care. Yes, I'll talk to Father. I'm sure he can help me."

"That's what I mean. You have courage! I'll be praying for you. My next class will be here in fifteen minutes. You may come to the library or magazine room any time today. I'll give you the day's pass. Just in case you need to be by yourself. I'm sure you can find a quiet spot," the teacher offered.

At least Greta was smiling and almost tearless when the sister left the room. The episode troubled the religious for a long time. She was comforted the following term, however, when Greta confided in Sister Mary that she had no trouble after the incident with Jack. Several young men had asked her to go to the prom.

After another short hospital stay, Amy's insurance discontinued coverage. It was suggested that she be transferred to a nursing home. Of course, family members were devastated. Visits to nursing homes assured them that if one could, those were places to avoid.

"Give up your apartment and come stay in Churchville," persuaded Patricia and Lucy. It was a good choice. There was enough room. There was a bathroom on the first floor next to the room the patient occupied and nurses' were hired when the need arrived. The youngest family member never showed signs of the pain and discomfort she felt. She did often worry that she might become a helpless burden.

It was not to be. It was a terminal illness that was devastating the young woman. She must have realized it even when she was in the happiest of moods. Sister Mary recalled the many times she engaged the religious in spiritual insights. Conversations would weave around the greatness of God's goodness, and the holiness of members of the family that had died. Amy and Lucy both liked candles and would often on impulse say,

"Let's light some candles and pray."

"Remember the times Grandma would tell us light a candle. It was time to pray," one of the women would comment. There always were candles in the Tantalo homes. With the passing of time they were becoming much more decorative and popular. Candlelight, thought Sister Mary, did often set the stage for quiet focus before praying.

The day Amy died was one of those beautiful spring sunny days. There was a nurse in attendance although her sisters were present. The patient had slept most of the day and after a brief period of consciousness with smiles and a few prayers, the nurse gave her medication. She just slept away.

All felt the loss very keenly. After all, she was the youngest in the family and such a delight to have around.

It shattered Lucy for almost a year. They had been inseparable as young children being the last two babies of the large family. It was Lucy who comforted Amy when her marriage became troubled. Those two women shared and sought each other's advice whenever difficulty loomed.

"Thank God for a hereafter. After all we now have another intercessor in heaven," family members would comfort after admitting there was a void that would not go away.

At the time that Amy's illness had become more advanced, Fred, the youngest brother, too, was stricken with a terminal illness. Francis, who often came to visit the sick members during the time remarked,

"He has a strange type of cancer. I'm sure it is the outcome of his activities in the Navy during World War Two.

No one comes out of the war unscathed. There are always penalties for the Navy man or soldier," added the oldest brother.

"That is true, I recall when Dom came for a short visit several years ago. He had come east to evaluate a company that was sending material to his place in California.

Remember when he had an eye blinking session? Francis, you asked him about his problem. Never before had he mentioned his stay at the Japanese prison camp. His captors put him to work at a steel furnace. Sparks could not be avoided. Prisoners were not given protective glasses. That was terrible," Patricia reminded the group.

"He also said that only a Japanese doctor knew how to treat the ailment. He could never approach a Japanese without rancor," added Francis.

Francis, the eldest brother, was always conscious of his responsibility as the big brother. This, perhaps, was an offshoot of European tradition. Frank, as family members called him, would travel to check on family. He didn't hesitate to go to California to visit Joseph and Dom. Only after his first heart attack did he curtail his travels. When the youngest boy and girl of the family fell ill, he frequently came to Rochester for quick visits. The youngest brother died December of the same year as Amy.

Family members visited Lucy often after Amy's death. Frank and Irene would come weekends and Irene, would urge Lucy to go antique hunting. Periodically, Lucy would return with them to the North Country. On these visits, Irene would drive Lucy around in search of items. Francis, never much sold on antiques, would remain at home. He referred to collectibles and antiques as other peoples' junk. In fact, one day when Irene came back with a flowery china chamber pot, he became incensed.

"That is not coming into our house. I'm not interested in ancient people's toilets," Frank remarked heatedly. Both women laughed at the comment. Irene made it a gift to her sister-in-law. It sold at a good profit, Lucy would laughingly tell Frank.

From then on, it was not uncommon for Sister Mary to receive phone calls that a family member became seriously ill. Irene was one of the first. She was stricken with a cancer that was constantly reoccurring. Much of the last ten years of her life were spent in and out of the hospital. Francis would often become agitated at the care she received. He finally moved her from the Malone hospital to the one in Plattsburg. He would make the long trips even if the roads were icy and treacherous.

On one Occasion, phoning Francis several days before the Thanksgiving holidays, Patricia and Lucy enquired about Irene's health.

"She is in the hospital in Plattsburg again," the brother replied.

"What are you going to do for Thanksgiving? We hear that you are snowed in," question Patricia.

"I am driving to Plattsburg as I do each day," answered Francis.

"You get yourself a room in a nearby hotel. Don't travel back and forth in this weather. With your heart problem, you should never attempt those long rides," scolded Patricia.

These were difficult times for surviving members of the Tantalo family. How quickly they were all getting stricken with illnesses. Sister Mary spent late night vigils in chapel praying for the needs of family, students and emerging social problems.

Demands of heavy scheduled days and students needing tools of research kept the teacher busy. The young people assured her often that they were praying for sick members of her family. The Religious was happy when working with students. They were not only stimulating but also caring.

On one of those days when she had just heard that her brother Dom in California was not well, students of her first period class were very much aware that something was troubling the religious. It happened to be Sister Stephanie's junior literature class. The teacher of the junior class mentioned it during the prayer session before the start of the period.

As they were leaving, one of the students said,

"Sister, please be here at two thirty, after the dismissal bell. You are going to receive an award," smiling said the student as he rushed out of the library. That afternoon, all students were filed around the room   against the bookshelves. At the signal from one of the boys, all reached above the top shelves and produced a trophy.

"We offer you all these trophies for being the best librarian."

Seriously and in unison proclaimed the group. The religious was really touched and almost tearful. She laughingly related the incident to the sisters at the Convent that evening.

The religious that worked in the school gathered for prayer and Mass in the morning and again for evening prayer. During the evening meal time when they met together as well as recreation period after supper were good times to discuss school events, family concerns or just plain chatter. These are choice times for most convent groups. Members of religious orders often relied on sisters of their own community to give them support and encouragement in their undertakings, problems and requests. School Sisters of Notre Dame that taught or worked in the Rochester area were always ready to lend a helping hand and meet the needs of their companions. Sister Mary was grateful to these groups of sisters that came to her aid when there was a serious illness in the Tantalo family.

An evening in mid -week, Sister Mary phoned her sister Fan. The following day was a school holiday. Frances spent most weekends in Churchville but she liked her small house not far from the city. The older sister liked to meet friends at McCurdy's Garden Room in the mid town area. She usually had lunch with some of her colleagues. Frances retired from home sales and worked in the Art department of a department store. She had a passion for music and art.

"You have tomorrow off. Why don't you meet me at four o'clock for supper in the Garden Room. It'll be my treat," offered Frances.

As was her custom, Sister Mary arrived shortly before four o'clock. She found a seat near the entrance and waited for her sister. Getting fidgety by four thirty, she phoned her sisters Patricia and Lucy.

"I was to meet Frances at four. She isn't at the Garden Room yet. I'm worried. I phoned her home and there is no answer," the religious alarmingly informed her sisters.

"I just phoned the Convent. Frances fell. She is at her neighbors. I was going to ask you to come to Fan's and we would take her to the hospital. Sister Clare suggested that since Fan is so near BK, she would hop into a car and check it out then phone us. Take a cab to Frances home. Clare is already on her way. Don't worry, I spoke to Fran. She said that she has very little pain but we will check with the doctor," answered Lucy.

The young Sister Clare, energetic and smiling already had phoned the doctor. He suggested that an ambulance take Frances to the hospital just in case the injury was serious.

Sister Mary rode along with Frances while Sister Clare, phoned the sisters in Churchville, locked the patient's house and arrived at the hospital emergency before the ambulance. Amazed with the efficiency and know how of the young sister, Patricia and Lucy were not only surprised but also relieved.

Once Frances was admitted and in a comfortable room, she asked for a newspaper and as was usual with Fan, suggested to the two religious,

"You have to teach in the morning. They won't do anything tonight and I'm sure I'll be having tests all of tomorrow. I'll phone the convent and give you the info. You will make a good superior some day, Sister Clare," she said and smilingly dismissed the sisters.

Francis needed surgery, did very well with her rehab and was ready to be discharged. The doctor suggested she find an apartment to live in. Sleeping quarters in her home were on the second floor. Patricia and Lucy tried to convince her to move in with them.

"Country living is too complicated for me. Some of my friends live in an adult home. That will be nice. No cooking, no garden work. I'll have time to read, listen to music and chat with friends. I'll still come to Churchville weekends," Frances assured her sisters.

Adult homes were coming into vogue. The Episcopal Adult home was founded by two churchwomen that lived in a large mansion. As friends joined them, the Church purchased it. It was a lovely thirty room resident with full medical staff and a caring administrator. Women from other denominations were also encouraged to live there. A Catholic priest came once a week for Mass and the pastor sent parishioners for prayer services. It was a fine arrangement for Frances. The monthly fees were high but well worth the services Frances assured her friends and family members.

Within two years, Patricia and Lucy noticed it took Frances great effort to move the walker. After questioning Fan as well as the doctor both revealed that their sister was very anemic and required surgery. Surgery was not a good choice. During her hospital stay, Dom died of a heart ailment and Francis was too sick to visit but phoned Fan every day until her death. She was a resident of the adult home for only two years. Within that period of time, her bank account dwindled to zero and sale of the house paid for medical bills.

Examining Frances assets as well as debts, the administrator of the Episcopal Home shared with the family,

"It is getting worse with each passing month. Health insurance and medical costs are rising at an exponential rate. People can no longer get old, retire and live comfortably on their hard earned savings. So many of the residents here, like your sister, have ample funds for years of survival, however, they just better not need health care."

Within the next two years, both Francis and Joseph had died. The Churchville home was no longer a place where family members gathered. The only survivors were the three women, Patricia, Lucy and Sister Mary. It was still a beautiful get away for Sister Mary. However, she agreed with her sisters that the place was much to big for just two women.

A two-year search for a smaller comfortable house in the Highland Avenue area yielded zero. Searching other neighborhoods, they finally found a house that was small but large enough for them. One of the drawbacks, it needed repairs and restoration. Lucy was enthusiastic but Patricia could not be convinced that it was ready to move into. The decision agreed to was, Patricia would rent an apartment and live there for a year. Lucy would move into the house along with their pets and renovate and restore it while living on the premise. Weekends were spent either at the apartment or at

Lucy's house. Both places had sufficient room for Sister Mary. She would frequently visit weekends.

Lucy, one of the youngest in the family, was energetic, enthusiastic and comparatively happy. Despite sorrowful events, she never hesitated to lend a helping hand to neighbors. Requests for assistance were never refused. Renovating the house took not one year but over two years.

Patricia often admonished the younger sister,

"Lucy, you work too hard. The house looks great, call it quits," would be the suggestion. Thanksgiving holidays arrived and the house was finally ready. Spring was the target day for moving. Lucy seemed especially tired that holiday. The three remaining Tantalo women decided it would be a quiet celebration for just themselves. Within a few weeks Lucy became so lethargic and exhausted that Patricia suggested she visit a doctor. Sister Mary, too, gave her the same advice.

"I'm fine. I'll have the whole winter to be very lazy," Lucy would reply.

She didn't have the whole winter. Within two weeks, she was hospitalized and died of heart failure a few days after Christmas. It shocked Patricia. Sister Mary understood Patricia's pain. Again, not only the nuns but also faculty members and students came to the rescue. Kevin, one of the young teachers immediately went to Patricia's apartment and spoke to the two women, Patricia and Sister Mary.

"Sister Mary, did you select the grave site yet?" he asked.

"Yes, I phoned and they have a plot ready," was the answer.

"I'll check it out before I return home. If you like, I'll be happy to prepare the prayer services for wake and funeral. I know Father Graf and am a member of the prayer committee of the Church too. The fellows from your video club would be honored to be pallbearers. They remember Lucy from the picnics.

Kevin not only helped with the immediate details of services but also selected a plot that was much more adequate.

"You want to have a double plot. Pat, you are going to need one some day. I think the spot I selected will be much more to your liking. It is easy to locate, close to the entrance of the cemetery, near to the path and among some beautiful flowering bushes," the teacher stated.

The Notre Dame Sisters were especially solicitous. Friends visited Patricia and she was constantly receiving invitations and phone calls. The void would be there and time alone would bring healing. Faith in God and the assurance of a better afterlife was the mainstay of the two remaining family members.

Concern that Patricia might be alone and ill one day, Sister Mary discussed the possibility with her sister.

"Pat, you do understand that if I become ill, I would go to our retirement home in Connecticut. What are your plans in case of illness?" enquired the nun.

"I'd consider an adult home or even a nursing home if need be," the woman assured her sister. "In fact, Violet and I have been thinking that we might consider an adult home soon. Chapel Oaks might be a good choice," continued Pat. Since there was no immediate need, life went on tranquilly for several years.

Junior high students became part of the BK School complex. These students would now also share the library. Sister Mary had completed her twenty-fifth year as director.

"I am getting too involved. More scheduled classes, introducing new programs and greater book selection ranges are going to be very involving. So little of my time is being spent in quiet private prayer periods. It's time for me to include intervals of free slots for prayer. I'm going to ask for part time next year," the nun shared with her colleague, Sister Stephanie.

After discussing the needed change with one of the Notre Dame councilors, a replacement was hired. The nun spent much more time with her sister. There were days that she continued to remain working at the library.

"How come you are on part time and still spend so much time at work," questioned Patricia.

"I need to use the computer for some of the work. Between tasks, I can just spend time relaxing there," the religious replied.

"I am sure you just continue working most of the time. I'll order a computer then there will be no need to go back and forth so often. It would be nice to have a computer for our use. It would come in handy," Patricia suggested. Frequently, Sister Mary would use it for BK library tasks to ease the burden of the newly trained library director.

Unexpectedly, Patricia had a hart attack. Several days following the episode, surgery was not only suggested but also recommended by several medical people. There was some hesitancy. Finally Patricia agreed to have the surgery. It would be serious with several weeks of careful monitoring.

Patricia was a member of Our Lady's Parish. Not only Sister Sheila, the outreach nun but also the Pastor came often to the hospital for visits. When Patricia had short lucid moments, she asked for Sister Mary. The nun spent her waking hours at the hospital. Three weeks silent presence on the part of Sister Mary, gave the nun time for deep reflection, prayer and meditation. It was difficult for this task and activity oriented person to be still for such long periods of time. On consideration, sister Mary pondered,

"After all these years in religious life, I should be very comfortable at prayer and silence. My contemplative nature has not been developed. I've spent too much time in secular studies, and a slave to energetic enterprises. It's time to do more scripture searching and religious literature reading."

Returning to her apartment, after her long hospital stay, made it inevitable that Sister Mary's teaching time should be terminated. Her days were spent with Patricia. This was not a difficult time for the nun. Although she planed to be her sisters care giver, giving was reversed. It was Patricia that did all the giving. Her serene and excepting of each day's afflictions would be brushed aside and followed by,

"Don't worry, Mary, it's OK. No big deal," she would smile and quickly reply. It was remarkable how each day was passed with such calm acceptance. Patricia continued to appreciate the little everyday small pleasures. She joyfully phoned friends, played cards, read and worked on puzzles. Amazingly, if she received a phone call from a troubled friend, her compassionate listening and brief encouraging words made the listener aware of true selflessness. Those last days with Pat were real treasures for Sister Mary.

At times when the two sisters spoke of spiritual matters, Patricia's final statement was,

"God is good, compassionate and kind. I'm sure He is not picky like us humans."

Like her life, death came with no lengthy demands. Medications were causing problems that put her into an unconscious state. Within a few days she quickly slipped from this life to join her loved ones. It was a late April sunny day. Several days after the funeral, Sister Mary was at Pat's apartment. As she watched the heavy sheets of rain splash against the living room picture window, Sister Mary, overcome with loneliness and sadness, glanced heavenward. Tearfully, she challenged her deceased with

"You left me here on earth all by myself. Now I have no family. I don't know what to do."

"You left us to go to the convent. Just go back," Sister Mary was sure they responded.

She immediately phoned the Notre Dame councilor,

"Sister, several years ago you suggested I retire. I'll do that now. I'm looking forward to quiet prayer times. I'll have time to praise and thank God, " the religious responded.